Palgrave Studies in Digital Business & Enabling Technologies

Series Editors
Theo Lynn
Irish Institute of Digital Business
DCU Business School
Dublin, Ireland

Pierangelo Rosati
J.E. Cairnes School of Business and Economics
University of Galway
Galway, Ireland

This multi-disciplinary series will provide a comprehensive and coherent account of cloud computing, social media, mobile, big data, and other enabling technologies that are transforming how society operates and how people interact with each other. Each publication in the series will focus on a discrete but critical topic within business and computer science, covering existing research alongside cutting edge ideas. Volumes will be written by field experts on topics such as cloud migration, measuring the business value of the cloud, trust and data protection, fintech, and the Internet of Things. Each book has global reach and is relevant to faculty, researchers and students in digital business and computer science with an interest in the decisions and enabling technologies shaping society. More information about this series at http://www.palgrave.com/gp/series/16004.

Theo Lynn • Pierangelo Rosati
Edel Conway • Lisa van der Werff
Editors

The Future of Work

Challenges and Prospects for Organisations, Jobs and Workers

palgrave
macmillan

Editors
Theo Lynn
Irish Institute of Digital Business
DCU Business School
Dublin City University
Dublin, Ireland

Pierangelo Rosati
J.E. Cairnes School of Business
and Economics
University of Galway
Galway, Ireland

Edel Conway
DCU Business School
Dublin City University
Dublin, Ireland

Lisa van der Werff
DCU Business School
Dublin City University
Dublin, Ireland

ISSN 2662-1282 ISSN 2662-1290 (electronic)
Palgrave Studies in Digital Business & Enabling Technologies
ISBN 978-3-031-31493-3 ISBN 978-3-031-31494-0 (eBook)
https://doi.org/10.1007/978-3-031-31494-0

This Palgrave Macmillan imprint is published by the registered company Springer Nature Switzerland AG.
The registered company address is: Gewerbestrasse 11, 6330 Cham, Switzerland

Acknowledgement

This book was funded by the Irish Institute of Digital Business at DCU Business School.

Book Description

The COVID-19 pandemic accelerated adoption of new forms of working and new working arrangements largely enabled by technology. The Future of Work is a projection of how work, working, workers and the workplace will evolve in the years ahead from the perspective of different actors in society, influenced by technological, socio-economic, political and demographic changes. This open access Pivot is a timely exploration of some of the challenges and prospects for the future of work from two main perspectives: how work is changing and how to prepare for work in the future. An evidence-based assessment of these topics offers some critical perspectives that challenge old assumptions and opens up emerging trends and possibilities for work in the future. Part of the Palgrave Studies in Digital Business & Enabling Technologies series, this book is an essential reference resource for academics of Business, Human Resource Management, Organisational Psychology and Industrial Relations, as well as practitioners and policy makers.

Contents

Notes on Contributors

Elisabeth E. Bennett is Associate Professor of Business and Director of the Master of Science in Leadership at Concordia University, Wisconsin and Ann Arbor. Dr. Bennett produced seminal work on virtual human resource development (VHRD), starting with her dissertation study completed at the University of Georgia in 2006. Additional research interests include technology, informal learning, organizational culture, and creativity. Dr. Bennett has served as a member of the Academy of Human Resource Development board. Dr. Bennett has substantial industry leadership experience in Fortune 500 financial services, manufacturing, and an executive role in academic medicine.

Caleb Bernacchio is Assistant Professor of Management and Ethics at California State University Monterey Bay. His research focuses on virtue ethics and organization theory. He has published in various business ethics, philosophy, and management journals.

Janine Bosak is Professor of Work and Organisational Psychology and Director of Research of the Leadership and Talent Institute (LTI) at Dublin City University. Her research interests lie in the areas of women and leadership, employee wellbeing in organisations, and culture.

Matej Černe is Associate Professor of Management at the School of Economics and Business, University of Ljubljana, Slovenia. His research interests include non-technological innovations, creativity, human resource management, leadership, bibliometrics, and digital work. He is currently managing a virtual platform for research dissemination #HumanizingDigitalWork.

Jeanette N. Cleveland is Full Professor Emeritus of Industrial and Organizational Psychology at Colorado State University, Department of Psychology. Her research includes aging at work gender and age bias in work decisions, and interface between work-nonwork and age/gender. She is an elected Fellow to the Society of Industrial/Organizational Psychology.

Edel Conway is Full Professor of HRM and Organisational Psychology and Associate Dean of Research at DCU Business School. Her research focuses on employee perspectives on work, particularly employee engagement and wellbeing and employee reactions to work intensification and organisational change. She was awarded a Fellowship of the Irish Academy of Management for her contribution to the advancement of management studies in Ireland.

Shirley Davey is Lecturer in Innovation and Management Development in Ulster University Business School. She is course Director for the New Transformational Management in a Digital World course funded by DfE. She has over 25 publications and is a reviewer for several journals in the fields of Technology and Management. She received the Award for 'Best Paper in Healthcare & Public Sector Management' from the Irish Academy of Management. Her PhD students are currently working on projects related to innovation education ecosystems and sustainable innovation for future growth.

James Duggan is Assistant Professor of Management and Organisational Behaviour at the School of Business, Maynooth University, Ireland. A previous Irish Research Council awardee, his research interests include technology-enabled HRM, algorithmic management, and work in the gig economy.

Orla Feeney is Associate Professor of Accounting at DCU Business School, Ireland. Her research focuses on the exploration of accounting as a social phenomenon within organisations, the impact of digital technology on accounting and the future of work in an accounting context.

Yseult Freeney is Professor of Organisational Psychology in DCU Business School and Research Director of the Irish Institute for Digital Business. Her research agenda is driven by a passionate interest in the well-being of employees and in helping them to thrive at work. Her research contributes to understanding how organisations can foster sustainable work engagement and work-life enrichment for employees against a backdrop of increasing work intensification and remote working, as well as a particular interest in how women navigate transitions at work.

Thomas N. Garavan is Professor of Leadership Practice in Cork University Business School, University College Cork and Visiting Research Professor, National College of Ireland, Dublin. He was recently listed in the Stanford University Science-Wide author citation indicators 2020 in the top 2% of academics in Economics and Business. He was ranked the top Irish Business and Management Researcher in Ireland by Research.com and 471 of 1500 business and management researchers worldwide in 2022. He is a world leading expert in leadership development, learning and development, and HRD. He has published 185 journal articles, 16 books, 26 book chapters and 6 monographs.

Claire Gubbins is Professor of Organisational Behaviour and HRM at Dublin City University, Ireland. Previously she was a Fulbright Scholar at Carnegie Mellon University, an Associate Editor for Human Resource Development Quarterly and a Senior Research Fellow on a University-Industry project on Tacit Knowledge Management and Learning. Her research centres on learning and knowledge circulation via social networks. Dr. Gubbins has co-authored two books: Learning and Development in Organisations: Strategy, Evidence and Practice with OakTree Press and Learning and Development Effectiveness in Organisations: An Integrated Systems-Informed Model of Effectiveness with Palgrave Macmillan.

Brian Harney is Professor of Strategy and HRM at DCU Business School. His recent co-edited collections include The Global HR Case Book (Routledge), Reframing HRM in SMEs (Palgrave Macmillan) and Protecting the Future of Work: New Institutional Arrangements for Safeguarding Labour Standards (Emerald). Brian was the 2020 recipient of the Academy of Management HR Division Innovative Educator award. He currently serves as Associate Editor for Human Resource Management and guest editor for special issues of IJHRM, HRM Review, International Small Business Journal and Employee Relations.

Stefan Jooss is Lecturer in Management and Programme Director for the Higher Diploma in Human Resource Management at Cork University Business School, University College Cork, Ireland. His main research interest and focus is in the areas of talent management, global mobility, and future of work. He also co-edited a book on Talent Management Innovations in the International Hospitality Industry.

Amadeja Lamovšek is a PhD student of the Business/Management track at the School of Economics and Business (SEB) of the University of Ljubljana, Slovenia. Her research interests include (digital) work design, human resource management, organizational behavior and psychology. Her academic profile is also highly practitioner-oriented, as she is active in various non-profit organisations and societies, and owns a business venture specialised in social media marketing and business consulting.

Theo Lynn is Full Professor of Digital Business at Dublin City University and Co-director of the Irish Institute of Digital Business. He was formerly the Principal Investigator (PI) of the Irish Centre for Cloud Computing and Commerce, and Director of the LINK Research Centre. Professor Lynn specialises in the role of digital technologies in transforming business processes and society with a specific focus on cloud computing, social media and data science.

Jean McCarthy is Lecturer in Organisational Behaviour at the University of Limerick. Jean is a former Fulbright Scholar at Colorado State University and Ambassador for the Fulbright Commission in Ireland. Her research centres on understanding organisational attitudes and behaviour which promote a more inclusive and sustainable workplace.

Kathy Monks is Emeritus Professor of HRM at DCU Business School. Her research interests include HR systems, work engagement, employee well-being and the future of work. Kathy was founder of the LINK Research Centre at Dublin City University and is a Fellow of the Irish Academy of Management.

Brid Murphy is Associate Professor of Accounting at DCU Business School, Ireland. Her principal research focuses on the impact of digital technology on the accounting profession, the role of accounting in society and the development of competence in the accounting profession.

Irina Nikolova is Assistant Professor of Organizational Behavior and HRM at the Department of Organisation, Strategy, and Entrepreneurship at Maastricht University, School of Business and Economics. Her research focuses on organisational change, including digitalised workplaces and employee adaptation, leadership (e.g., engaging leadership, leader-member exchange), organisational climate (e.g., learning climate, job insecurity climate) and smart cities.

Emma Parry is Professor of Human Resource Management and Head of the Changing World of Work Group at Cranfield School of Management, United Kingdom. Her research focuses on the impact of the changing external context on managing people, particularly in relation to national context, workforce demographics and technological advancement.

Marta Rocchi is Assistant Professor of Corporate Governance and Business Ethics at DCU Business School and member of the Irish Institute of Digital Business. Her research focuses on virtue ethics in business and finance, the new perspectives of business ethics in the future of work, and the ethical dilemmas of the digital world.

Pierangelo Rosati is Associate Professor of Digital Business and Society at University of Galway. His research interests include digital business, business value of IT, FinTech, Blockchain, cloud computing, and cyber security.

Simon Daniel Schafheitle is Assistant Professor of Human Resource Management and Artificial Intelligence at the University of Twente. His research focuses on understanding twenty-first-century workplace architectures as an interplay of datafication control and trust. In doing so, he focuses on how technology impacts control configurations and how heightened states of vulnerability and threats to experienced meaningfulness of work can be overcome.

Lisa van der Werff is Associate Professor of Organisational Psychology and Director of Doctoral Studies at DCU Business School. Her research focuses on trust in interpersonal, organisational and human-technology relationships. She is Co-director of Irish Institute of Digital Business and President of an international network of trust researchers (FINT; www.fintweb.org), and sits on the editorial board of Human Relations and Journal of Trust Research.

Sut I. Wong is Professor and Head of Department of Communication and Culture at BI Norwegian Business School. In addition, Sut I is a Professor II at University of Oslo and an adjunct faculty at University of

Ljubljana. Sut I was a co-founder of the Nordic Centre for Internet and Society at BI. Sut I's research interests center on new ways of working, digital teams, team innovation, and managing digital transformation.

Xuchang Zheng is Assistant Professor of Organisational Behaviour and Chair of MSc in Human Resource Management at DCU Business School. Xuchang's research focuses on the process of trust development and decline, examining the influence of cognitive biases on people's trust decisions.

List of Figures

List of Tables

CHAPTER 1

Introducing the Future of Work: Key Trends, Concepts, Technologies and Avenues for Future Research

Theo Lynn, Pierangelo Rosati, Edel Conway, and Lisa van der Werff

Abstract The Future of Work is a projection of how work, working, workers and the workplace will evolve in the years ahead from the perspective of different actors in society, influenced by technological, socio-economic, political and demographic changes. In addition to defining the Future of Work, this chapter discusses some of the main trends, themes

T. Lynn (✉)
Irish Institute of Digital Business, DCU Business School,
Dublin City University, Dublin, Ireland
e-mail: theo.lynn@dcu.ie

E. Conway • L. van der Werff
DCU Business School, Dublin City University, Dublin, Ireland
e-mail: edel.conway@dcu.ie; lisa.vanderwerff@dcu.ie

P. Rosati
J.E. Cairnes School of Business and Economics, University of Galway,
Galway, Ireland
e-mail: pierangelo.rosati@universityofgalway.ie

T. Lynn et al. (eds.), *The Future of Work*, Palgrave Studies in Digital Business & Enabling Technologies,
https://doi.org/10.1007/978-3-031-31494-0_1

and concepts in the Future of Work literature before discussing the different topics covered in the remainder of the book. The chapter concludes with a call for greater inter- and multidisciplinary research, evidence to validate assumptions and hypotheses underlying extant Future of Work research and policy, greater use of futures methodologies and a future of research agenda that is even in its coverage of workspaces, population and employment cohorts, regions, sectors, and organisation types.

Keywords Future of Work • Technology • Digital technologies • Digital transformation • Artificial Intelligence

1.1 Introduction

The Future of Work is not a new idea; however, following the Covid-19 pandemic, it has become not only a major discourse in all aspects of life but a central pillar of government policy worldwide. The pandemic has mainstreamed a plethora of terms (see Table 1.2) for how we work in a post-Covid world—hybrid working, remote working and co-working are just some of artefacts that have travelled from the Future of Work to the now of work.

The Future of Work is both a short-term and long-term concern, and while central to industrial strategy, it is by no means limited to this domain. This is particularly evidenced in the European Union where the Future of Work plays a central role in the updated European Industrial Strategy and the European Pillar of Social Rights Action Plan, and is a field of action for the European Research Area and its policy agenda (European Commission, 2022). At the time of writing, the European Commission has invested *c.* €1.9 billion in areas related to the Future of Work, including research and innovation, economic competitiveness and social protection measures (European Commission, 2022). It should not be a surprise therefore that the Future of Work is of significant interest to scholars. Despite this interest, it would seem to be something everybody understands but nobody can explain.

This chapter seeks to provide greater clarity on what the Future of Work is or might be. The remainder of the chapter begins with a discussion on the definition of the Future of Work and proposes a working definition for the purposes of this book. This is followed by a brief overview of key trends, themes and concepts on the Future of Work before providing an overview of the topics discussed in the remaining chapters of this book. We conclude with a discussion on some potential future avenues for research and highlight the need for inter- and multidisciplinary research, evidence to validate the many assumptions and hypotheses underlying extant Future of Work research and policy, greater use of futures methodologies and a future of research agenda that is even in its coverage of population and employment cohorts, regions, sectors, workspaces and organisation types.

1.2 What Is the Future of Work?

The term "Future of Work" in itself poses at least three significant challenges for researchers, practitioners and policymakers alike. Firstly, the study of the future requires boundaries. Predicting the future in the social sphere is particularly difficult as there are no strong laws (as in the sciences), and identifying and aggregating relevant information is complicated by its dispersal across different people and organisations (Chen et al., 2003). In particular, one needs to be careful not to fall foul of the so-called futures fallacies (Dorr, 2017). Thus, any future projection should not:

- assume a simple and steady extension of past trends (linear projection fallacy);
- consider only one single aspect of change while holding "all else equal" (*ceteris paribus* fallacy); and
- envision possible futures as static objects rather than as a dynamic process, an ongoing procession of changes (the arrival fallacy) (Dorr, 2017).

The second challenge relates to what we mean when we say "work." A quick review of the literature will reveal that when we talk about the Future of Work it may be related to a particular activity (what), the process of working (how), the worker (who) and the workplace (where), or any combination of these. Thirdly, the Future of Work can be viewed from a variety of perspectives from macro to micro, from a society, industry, firm or an individual level (Stoepfgeshoff, 2018).

When dealing with the future, it is always a movable feast. The Future of Work is not new but rather is the latest iteration of an established phenomenon where the current wave of interest is largely driven by the impact of Covid-19 on accelerating technology adoption and new flexible work arrangements. To paraphrase Webster (2006), there is both change and persistence.

Given its prominence in the public discourse, it is unsurprising that increasingly scholars are arriving at the conclusion that there is no clear understanding about what the Future of Work is (Stoepfgeshoff, 2018;

Santana & Cobo, 2020). The scholarly literature is remarkably scarce on precise definitions of the Future of Work. Instead, the literature on the Future of Work is defined by characteristics or narratives. This is even a feature of reviews of Future of Work research. For example, Balliester and Elsheikhi (2018) define the Future of Work along five dimensions in which changes brought about by megatrends such as technology, climate change, globalisation and demography impact the world of work, namely (1) the future of jobs; (2) the quality of jobs; (3) wage and income inequality; (4) social protection systems; and (5) social dialogue and industrial relations. Mitchell et al. (2022) do not define the Future of Work but categorise the most influential research into four key research streams: (1) workplace relations, (2) workplace change, (3) diversity and (4) personal skills. Similarly, in their review, Kolade and Owoseni (2022) do not define the Future of Work but rather identify three underlying theoretical perspectives from the literature, namely (1) socio-technical systems theory, (2) skill-biased technological change and (3) political economy of automation and digital transformation.

This is not to say that there are no definitions but perhaps one must look elsewhere, for example, to practice. Gartner (2022) defines the Future of Work as "[…] the changes in how work will get done over the next decade, influenced by technological, generational and social shifts." The Society for Human Resource Management (SHRM) defines the Future of Work as "a projection of how work, workers and the workplace will evolve in the years ahead" (SHRM, 2022). In the same vein, Deloitte defines the Future of Work as "encompass(ing) changes in work, the workforce, and the workplace" (Schwartz et al., 2019). While Gartner (2022) puts a specific, albeit moving, time horizon of ten years, both Gartner (2022) and SHRM (2022) include a consideration of a time still to come unlike Schwartz et al. (2019). However, while Gartner's definition focuses exclusively on how work (the what) will be done in the future, the SHRM and Deloitte definitions are wider including how workers (the who) and the workplace (the where) will evolve. Moreover, Gartner recognises that the Future of Work is impacted by the outside world and accommodates these shifts. None of these definitions recognise that the Future of Work may be inflected by the actor perspective. As such, for the purposes of this book, we propose the following definition of the Future of Work which accommodates these existing definitions as well as important dimensions recognised in scholarly literature, namely technological, socio-economic, political and demographic changes (Balliester & Elsheikhi, 2018; Anner et al., 2019; Santana & Cobo, 2020; Mitchell et al., 2022):

The Future of Work is a projection of how work, working, workers and the workplace will evolve in the years ahead from the perspective of different actors in society, influenced by technological, socio-economic, political, and demographic changes.

1.3 Key Trends, Themes and Concepts in the Future of Work

Based on our discussion on the definitions of the Future of Work, it is clear that extant thinking is heavily inflected by a number of predominant trends, themes, concepts and technologies which can be viewed at different levels of granularity. At a high level, technology, climate change, globalisation and demographic changes are common megatrends cited in the literature (Balliester & Elsheikhi, 2018). At a more granular level, the focus breaks out into a wide range of trends—the impact of restructuring on efficiency including supply chain optimisation and outsourcing, ageing populations, increased migration and mobility, greater emphasis on work-life balance and wellness, amongst others. More recently, of course, the role and impact of Covid-19, and indeed, future pandemics, has become more prominent and is likely to remain part of the discourse for some time.

In a recent article, Paul Deane (2021) said: "when thinking about the future, we often overemphasise the role of technology and underestimate where technology fits in a social context." This has undoubtedly been true in the case of the Future of Work. The predominant theme of literature, from the academy, industry and policymakers, has focussed on the implications of greater digitalisation, automation and analytics on the Future of Work. Unsurprisingly, much of this discourse focuses on advancements in Artificial Intelligence (AI) and associated labour-market and societal effects, although more often than not the distinction between narrow task-focussed AI and more wide-ranging artificial general intelligence (AGI) is ignored.

Academia is neither ignorant of these trends nor deaf to concerns. In their recent review of the 32 most influential publications in the field, Mitchell et al. (2022) categorise the research into four themes. These are further subdivided into 11 sub-themes—workplace relations (well-being, job insecurity, grievance process, mentoring); workplace changes (evolution of the workplace, telecommuting); diversity (workplace diversity, gender diversity, age discrimination) and personal skills (people skills and storytelling). Echoing Dorr (2017), it is important to remember that

Future of Work research merely provides "snapshots of an inherently dynamic process." Santana and Cobo (2020) discuss the thematic evolution of Future of Work research over four periods from 1959 to 2019 based on a systematic mapping of 2286 documents, which is largely consistent with Mitchell et al. (2022). These are summarised in Table 1.1. While it is clear that specific perspectives, fears, insights and recommendations are of their age, there are also persistent themes (e.g., telework) and themes that go in and out of vogue (e.g., employment).

In addition to thematically analysing the evolution of Future of Work research, Santana and Cobo (2020) further categorise themes into four dimensions—technological, social, economic and political/institutional. Technologies such as automation, digitalisation, platformisation and AI are both creating new forms of work (e.g., gig working) and enabling flexible work arrangements (e.g., hybrid, remote and shared working) (Santana & Cobo, 2020). Furthermore, AI is introducing new forms of management through algorithmic management, which in turn require new types of skills to train, monitor and optimise such tools. Key terms and concepts in the Future of Work are presented in Table 1.2.

Table 1.1 Evolution of key themes in Future of Work research 1959–2019 (adapted from Santana & Cobo, 2020)

Period	*Motor Themes*	*Emerging and Specialised Themes*
1959–1997	• Employment • Organisational Change • Experiences (incl. reemployment and layoffs)	
1998–2008	• Telework • New Organisational Forms	• Wage (In)equality (incl. discrimination, technological change and skills)
2009–2014	• Telework • Electronic Human Resource Management • Wage (In)equality	• Migrant and Older Workers • Talent Management • Job Satisfaction • Innovation
2015–2019	• Wage (In)equality • Telework • Satisfaction • Talent Management	• Employment • Careers • Innovation • Organisational Commitment • Older Workers • Corporate Social Responsibility • Automation • Leadership • Vulnerable Workers

Table 1.2 Key terms and concepts in the Future of Work

Term	*Definition*
Activity-based Working	In activity-based working, "workers do not have assigned workstations, but instead share an office space offering different types of non-assigned work settings, which are intended to be used for different types of activities" (Hoendervanger et al., 2016).
Algorithm	An algorithm is a set of rules that must be followed when solving a particular problem (Oxford English Dictionary, 2022).
Algorithmic Management	Software algorithms that assume managerial functions and surrounding institutional devices that support algorithms in practice (Lee et al., 2015). Algorithmic management relies heavily on data collection and surveillance of workers to enable automated or semi-automated decision-making (Mateescu & Nguyen, 2019).
Artificial Intelligence (AI)	The capability of a machine to engage in cognitive activities performed by a human brain (UNCTAD, 2021).
Artificial General Intelligence (AGI)	Systems that possess a reasonable degree of self-understanding and autonomous self-control and have the ability to solve a variety of complex problems in a variety of contexts and to learn to solve new problems that they didn't know about at the time of their creation (Goertzel & Pennachin, 2007).
Augmented Reality (AR)	A type of virtual reality in which synthetic stimuli are superimposed on real-world objects usually to make information that is otherwise imperceptible to human senses perceptible (Department of Defense, 1998).
Co-working	Co-working refers to the co-localisation of a group of individuals with more or less heterogeneous backgrounds in the same work environment (Kojo & Nenonen, 2016). Co-working spaces involve three primary concepts: telecentres, serviced offices and co-working spaces (Kojo & Nenonen, 2017).
Extended Reality (XR)	Extended Reality (XR) refers to applications that blend the digital and the physical worlds in different ways: both by situating virtual worlds into physical environments by means of augmented and mixed reality technologies, and by exploiting smart things and devices in the physical environment connected to the virtual world, in a pervasive computing perspective (Croatti & Ricci, 2020).
Gig Work(ing)	Externalised paid work organised around "gigs" (i.e., projects or tasks) that workers engage in on a term-limited basis without a formal appointment within a particular organisation (Caza et al., 2022).
Gig Economy	The intermediation of labour typically via an online platform that matches workers with those who require work to be done on a per service basis (Lynn et al., 2022; Schwellnus et al., 2019).

(*continued*)

Table 1.2 (continued)

Term	*Definition*
Hoffices	Coined by futurist Faith Popcorn to describe a home-office, it can also refer to a self-organising network that brings together people who wish to co-create temporary workplaces, often in each other's homes (Rossitto et al., 2017).
Hybrid Working	A work arrangement in which employees combine working from an employing organisation's worksite and some other location.
Machine Learning (ML)	A computational method that makes use of experience in the form of input data to achieve a desired task without being literally programmed (i.e., "hard coded") to produce a particular outcome (El Naqa & Murphy, 2015).
Metaverse	Initially conceptualised as a world where virtual and reality interact and create value through various social activities (Stephenson, 1992), the term is also used to refer to a topology for multiple virtual worlds (Dionisio et al., 2013).
Mirror Worlds	Mirror worlds are digital creations that mimic the physical and social structures of the real world in a virtual reality setting (Anderson & Rainie, 2022).
Mixed Reality (MR)	A subclass of virtual reality-related technologies that involve the merging of real and virtual worlds (Milgram & Kishino, 1994).
Narrow Artificial Intelligence	Software programmes that demonstrate intelligence in one or another specialised area (Goertzel & Pennachin, 2007).
Platformisation	The penetration of infrastructures, economic processes and governmental frameworks of digital platforms in different economic sectors and spheres of life, as well as the reorganisation of cultural practices and imaginations around these platforms (Poell et al., 2019).
Remote Working	A work arrangement in which the employee resides and works at a location beyond the local commuting area of the employing organisation's worksite (Allen et al., 2015).
Shared Working	Shared working, also referred to as job sharing or work sharing, is an employment arrangement where two people, or sometimes more, are retained on a part-time or reduced-time basis to perform a job normally fulfilled by one person working full-time (Mohamed, 2012).
Telecommuting	Working some portion of time away from the conventional workplace, often from home, and communicating by way of computer-based technology (Allen et al., 2015).
Telepresence	A situation where a person is objectively present in a real environment that is physically separate from the person in space (Schloerb, 1995).

(*continued*)

Table 1.2 (continued)

Term	*Definition*
Teleworking	A work practice that involves members of an organisation substituting a portion of their typical work hours (ranging from a few hours per week to nearly full-time) to work away from a central workplace—typically principally from home—using technology to interact with others as needed to conduct work task (Allen et al., 2015).
Virtual Reality	Also known as virtual environment and virtual world, an environment represented by models and simulations. This environment is interactive, allowing the participant to look and navigate about the environment, enhancing the immersion effect (Department of Defense, 1998).

The transformative effect of technologies, and specifically digital technologies, on how society operates and how social actors interact with each other is well-documented and much-discussed (Martin, 2008; Reis et al., 2018; Lynn et al., 2022). The technological impact on work has a knock-on effect on individuals and citizens. There are real and serious concerns about how new forms of work and working arrangements affect the social dimension of the Future of Work (Santana & Cobo, 2020) and social cohesion more generally (Anner et al., 2019). While benefitting some parts of society, innovations such as remote working and gig working may exacerbate other social problems and anxieties such as work-life conflict and burnout, as well as other outcomes including career development and progression and job satisfaction (Santana & Cobo, 2020). Weil (2014) has argued that innovations such as the gig economy can result in "fissured workplaces" where the bulk of employees are no longer central to the operation of the company due to outsourcing, franchising, and supply chain optimisation. Furthermore, the adoption of algorithmic management and other analytical techniques for employee surveillance while improving efficiency, performance and productivity may have adverse effects on employee voice and individual autonomy (Anner et al., 2019; Figueroa, 2018). Weil (2014), Anner et al. (2019), ILO (2017) and others argue that such advancements may, if not checked, result in a decline in wages and working conditions, while increasing levels of precarity and vulnerability experienced by workers. In contrast, Willcocks (2020), while suggesting that there will be considerable workforce and skill disruption due to technological advancements, suggests that claims on net job loss are exaggerated. Indeed, he argues that not only do extant studies fail to factor in dramatic increases in the amount of work to be done, they also fail to consider ageing populations, productivity gaps and skills shortages. Increasingly, this view is finding increasing support from several leading academics (Bessen et al., 2020; Malone et al., 2020).

The social and economic dimensions of work are inexplicably linked. When discussing the economic dimension of the Future of Work, the impact is different whether taking the perspective of the economy, sector, the firm or the individual worker. While technological advancements and increased efficiency, performance and productivity have a significant positive impact for economies and firms, the extant Future of Work literature highlights some major risks related to employment, wage inequality and job polarisation (Anner et al., 2019). As discussed, the impact of automation, robotics and AI on job numbers and wages is a significant topic of debate. Undoubtedly, some jobs will be replaced and some tasks automated, but equally new jobs and tasks will be created and to some extent AI will augment human capabilities (Bessen, 2018; Malone et al., 2020). Some commentators highlight some of the serious risks that a more globalised, gig- and remote working future might present to ensuring decent working conditions, minimum standards for workers and social cohesion (Anner et al., 2019). For example, Balliester and Elsheikhi (2018) note that the combination of labour-market changes and technological trends represent at least eight risks to existing working conditions. These include flexibility in hours and location, short-term and casual contracts, longer working hours, low pay and payment uncertainty, reduced occupational safety and health policies, dissolution of workers' organisation and bargaining power, erosion and absence of legal protection, and informality (Balliester & Elsheikhi, 2018).

"The future is already here, it's just not evenly distributed," a quote ascribed to the American science-fiction writer, William Gibson, foreshadows a key aspect of the discourse on the Future of Work and particularly the unevenness of the potential impact of technology on work (see, for example, Bessen, 2018 and Malone et al., 2020). Managing the adoption, and associated disruption, of these transformative technologies requires policymakers, political institutions and organisations to develop new organisational forms, policies and regulations to support and incentivise socially responsible adoption and use (Santana & Cobo, 2020; Willcocks, 2020), but also to retrain and transition workers to new occupations (Bessen, 2018; Malone et al., 2020; Mindell & Reynolds, 2022). This requires a significant multi-stakeholder effort and investment not only to train and upskill the workforce of the future and avoid potential skills inequities but to reduce adverse effects from disruption to longstanding societal norms and expectations. It may require not only a re-imagination of work but education, social protection, regulations and the role of institutions in the design and safeguarding the Future of Work. Given the delicate balance between social and economic policy, and the wide range of stakeholders affected by the Future of Work, governments need to consult and liaise with all stakeholders. This should not be limited to employers and labour organisations but should include the public, community organisations, education providers, data protection authorities and civil liberties advocates as early and transparently as possible so that suitable governance mechanisms are put in place to provide not only input but oversight on Future of Work initiatives.

1.4 Perspectives on the Future of Work

The nine remaining chapters in this book provide perspectives and insights that advance our understanding and help make sense of the Future of Work. They demonstrate that while there has been substantial intellectual effort in the conceptualisation of the Future of Work, we are still at an early stage in theorisation, exploratory and explanatory research, and more importantly actionable outcomes for practice. They are presented as follows.

Chapters 2 and 3 are dedicated to the impact of the increasing adoption of digital technologies in the workplace on employees' well-being and professions, respectively. More specifically, Chap. 2 focuses on new ways of working (NWW) which are defined as work practices that are enabled by complex information systems and virtualised organisational formations. The authors adopt self-determination theory (SDT) as a lens to explore the impact of NWW on three employees' universal needs, namely autonomy, competence and relatedness and the actual and potential implications for employees' well-being. The findings of this review suggest that relatedness is set to play a critical role in supporting the needs for autonomy and competence in increasingly digital workplaces.

Chapter 3 responds to an ongoing and growing debate on how professional roles are impacted and somewhat threatened by technology. This chapter looks at two professions that have been listed by the World Economic Forum (2018) among the most "at risk," namely accounting and law, and how they may be impacted by the shift from process and knowledge-oriented activities as a result of the adoption of AI and data analytics. The authors point out that professionals do not always face "standard" situations that can be solved using predetermined rules. On the contrary, most cases require individual professionals to make decisions based on their own judgement; this cannot and should not be replaced by an algorithm. The authors argue that while advancements in digital technologies can supplement and support human judgement, professionals must continue to apply autonomy and reflexive considerations to form independent judgments.

Chapter 4 turns the attention to the so-called gig-economy and related flexible and contingent forms of working that are enabled by digital platforms. More specifically, this chapter delves into how "gig-work" organisations have developed digitally enabled control systems that leverage AI and Machine Learning (ML) to manage their workforce. While the use of algorithmic management provides clear benefits for digital platforms in terms of higher efficiency and lower risks and labour costs, it also creates challenges for management practices, legislators and policymakers, as well as for workers. These challenges are discussed in more detail in the chapter, but they essentially point to the fact that the perceived independence from managerial control that is typical of gig work does not necessarily result in increased autonomy for workers and that closer attention needs to be paid to a number of aspects of gig work, such as the lack of various forms of support, that may detrimental for both gig workers and organisations.

Trust is arguably the cornerstone of any work relationship and the foundation of any social interaction. The increasing use of digital technologies, particularly those systems that leverage advancements in AI and ML, is likely to change the trust dynamics between employees and the organisation. This is the topic of Chap. 5, which is built on the argument that common practices of advocating the benefits and strengths of new technology are unlikely to be effective in building/protecting employees' trust as they fall short when it comes to supporting perceptions of organisational character or capability. The authors identify and discuss various challenges posed by the use of smart technology in the workplace (e.g., automation of leadership) and highlight a number of pathways to maximise the benefits of smart technology without undermining organisational trust.

Chapter 6 is dedicated to the role of leadership in the Future of Work. Leadership heavily relies on a leader's social presence which consists of three dimensions, namely co-presence, behavioural engagement and psychological involvement. While there is an extensive body of research exploring the factors that affect any of these three dimensions, little is known about how leadership dynamics change in a virtual and distributed workplace. The authors present a review of academic literature on leadership and the Future of Work and highlight and discuss four underexplored areas which represent avenues for future research, namely leadership in the context of virtual teams, leader-follower relationships in a digital workplace, the development of human and social capital in the digital world, and leadership in the platform-mediated economy. The authors point out the need for organisations' leaders to pay closer attention to both the range of digital technologies available and how these can be used to achieve organisational goals.

One of the main consequences of increasing globalisation is the growing diversity of the workforce in terms of race, ethnicity, gender, age, religion, culture, nationality and language. In addition to this, the use of digital technologies has facilitated the implementation of virtual and distributed teams implying that many organisations no longer have a dominant, traditional or homogenous pool of workers, nor do they have universal structures or approaches to work and working time. This poses both opportunities and challenges for organisations and these are presented and discussed in Chap. 7. The authors argue that the combination of a more diverse workforce, organisational leaders who are more aware of detrimental discriminatory attitudes and behaviour, and digital technologies that can transform the nature of work provides organisations with a unique opportunity to rethink their definition of success and what roles individual workers can play within the organisation to help organisations succeed.

The adoption of digital technologies not only changes how and where people work but also the skills required to play an active role in the digital economy and how these skills are acquired and developed. Chapters 8 and 9 discuss the learning aspects of the Future of Work. Chapter 8 delves into key skills required for the Future of Work and explores how these skills can be developed and co-created through formal yet flexible higher education and the potential impact this may have on the higher education system. The authors first outline the growing demand and pressure coming from the evolution of work and how this is affecting the higher education system and then highlight the need for universities to move away from a technical focus on skill development to a more holistic view of human-centred development. To conclude, the authors argue that higher education institutions should focus on providing students with innate capabilities and strategic awareness which will help them to identify and ask the right questions, to think critically, to explore silences and inequities, and to seek their own wisdom. In so doing, universities will prepare students for the various "futures of work" that they may be facing rather than a predetermined Future of Work that is based on current fixed disciplinary knowledge and predetermined career trajectories.

Chapter 9 discusses the role of digital technologies in the context of human resource development, specifically their role in learning and development (L&D). In this chapter, the authors highlight how, despite the growing attention received over the last few years and particularly during the Covid-19 pandemic, digital learning is still defined in a rather general all-encompassing way in the L&D literature. They provide an overview of L&D technology-based applications that would fall under this definition (e.g., AI, augmented and virtual reality, analytics, learning management systems, etc.) and describe their current use in this field. The authors then discuss how the drive for shorter, faster and less costly training and learning methods may undermine learning quality if digital learning methods are not designed with learning pedagogy in mind and call out the need for further research on synchronous and informal digital learning capabilities and effectiveness before conclusions can be reached concerning the effectiveness of digital learning in the context of human resource development.

Finally, Chap. 10 is dedicated to ethical considerations for the Future of Work. It considers how the adoption of digital technologies generates a new set of ethical questions regarding their contribution to workers' personal flourishing and to the good of society. In this chapter the authors argue that there is a need for an agent-centred approach to ethics, based on goods, norms and virtues, to analyse the ethical implications of digital technologies on the Future of Work.

1.5 Conclusions and Future Avenues for Research

This chapter introduces some of the challenges with Future of Work research, not least the lack of common definition in the scholarly literature. To address this gap, we define the Future of Work as "a projection of how work, working, workers, and the workplace will evolve in the years ahead from the perspective of different actors in society, influenced by technological, socio-economic, political and demographic changes." While we summarise the key trends, themes and concepts in the literature, this is largely from a social science perspective. Given that technology, and specifically digitalisation, automation, robotics and AI, is the predominant theme in the Future of Work discourses, we call for more inter- and multidisciplinary collaboration so that a more nuanced discourse on the impact of specific technologies or types of technologies on both jobs and tasks emerges. In particular, with the exception of a relatively small number of authors (see, for example, Malone et al., 2020 and Selenko et al., 2022), the differences between narrow AI and artificial general intelligence are under-appreciated and consequently under-researched.

The increased acceptance of new forms of working including remote working, hybrid working and other forms of teleworking during the Covid-19 pandemic has led to a renewed interest in where work is performed and how this may impact the design of workspaces. During the pandemic, work was increasingly performed in spaces beyond the commuting distance to the employer's work site, typically in their homes. However, there were notable increases in workers not only working remotely in holiday accommodation but also co-working spaces. In some instances, these co-working spaces were other workers' homes although not necessarily workers of the same employer (Rossitto et al., 2017). This so-called hoffice network phenomenon, in itself, may provide significant opportunities for future research. Contemporaneously, there has been a surge in interest in how extended reality (XR) technologies in all its various forms can be applied to work. Technologies such as virtual reality (VR), augmented reality (AR), mixed reality (MR), telepresence and mirror worlds have the potential to transform how we conceptualise workers and workspaces but also how we train, reskill and transition workers (see, for example, Anderson & Rainie, 2022). We encourage researchers to consider how these new technologies and workspaces impact how workers conceptualise where and how they perform work and the implications for workspace design, social interactions, management and organisational forms, amongst others.

Given the size and scope of the book, each chapter provides only a selected snapshot of a given topic. Notwithstanding this, each chapter identifies a potentially rich vein of research to validate or invalidate the hypotheses and arguments made to support a given academic or policy position. This does not mean one should be bound to the arguments of today and the timeline of the future. While there is an increasingly mature set of tools in social sciences for conceptualising the future, these are often not employed in scholarly research on the Future of Work or rather social science research, to echo Bainbridge (2003), is constrained by methodological rigour or value commitments. Thus, we call for not only greater use of futures methodologies but also research across more specific and longer-term time horizons. For policymakers, in particular, this will enable greater consideration of actionable interventions that can be taken within a more realistic timeframe.

Future of work literature, like much scholarly research, is often led by the more developed countries often focussing on the larger and more advanced commercial entities worldwide. This is particularly the case when discussing technological innovation and disruption. Small and medium-sized enterprises represent approximately 90% of businesses and more than 50% of employment worldwide and even higher in rural areas (World Bank, 2021). The Future of Work will impact different regions, sectors and organisation types in different ways and at different time scales. Similarly, the changes brought about by the Future of Work will impact different demographics and population cohorts, directly and indirectly, at different times. Successful adoption of new forms of work, workplaces or working arrangements is likely to depend on the worker's mindset at a given time. Accordingly, we call on researchers to ensure that Future of Work research is equally distributed across population demographics and cohorts, regions, sectors and organisation types.

Earlier in this chapter, we described the Future of Work as a movable feast characterised by persistence and change. For each generation, there is a new generation of Future of Work research, and for each Future of Work scholar, to borrow from Chambers (2010), a "cornucopia of potentials."

References

Allen, T. D., Golden, T. D., & Shockley, K. M. (2015). How effective is telecommuting? Assessing the status of our scientific findings. *Psychological Science in the Public Interest, 16*(2), 40–68.

Anderson, J., & Rainie, L. (2022). *The Metaverse in 2040.* Pew Research Center.

Anner, M., Pons-Vignon, N., & Rani, U. (2019). For a future of work with dignity: A critique of the World Bank Development Report, the changing nature of work. *Global Labour Journal, 10*(1), 2–19.

Bainbridge, W. S. (2003). The future in the social sciences. *Futures, 35*(6), 633–650.

Balliester, T., & Elsheikhi, A. (2018). The future of work: A literature review. *ILO Research Department Working Paper, 29*, 1–54.

Bessen, J. (2018). Artificial intelligence and jobs: The role of demand. In *The economics of artificial intelligence: An agenda* (pp. 291–307). University of Chicago Press.

Bessen, J., Goos, M., Salomons, A., & van den Berge, W. (2020). *Automation: A guide for policymakers.* Economic Studies at Brookings Institution.

Caza, B. B., Reid, E. M., Ashford, S. J., & Granger, S. (2022). Working on my own: Measuring the challenges of gig work. *Human Relations, 75*(11), 2122–2159.

Chambers, R. (2010). Paradigms, poverty and adaptive pluralism. *IDS Working Papers, 2010*(344), 1–57.

Chen, K. Y., Fine, L. R., & Huberman, B. A. (2003). Predicting the future. *Information Systems Frontiers, 5*(1), 47–61.

Croatti, A., & Ricci, A. (2020). From virtual worlds to mirror worlds: A model and platform for building agent-based extended realities. In *Multi-agent systems and agreement technologies* (pp. 459–474). Springer.

Deane, P. (2021). *Just why is it so hard to predict the future?* RTE Brainstorm. https://www.rte.ie/brainstorm/2019/0715/1062197-just-why-is-it-so-hard-to-predict-the-future/

Department of Defense. (1998). *DoD modeling and simulation glossary.* United States Department of Defense.

Dionisio, J., Burns, W., III, & Gilbert, R. (2013). 3D virtual worlds and the metaverse: Current status and future possibilities. *ACM Computing Surveys (CSUR), 45*(3), 1–38.

Dorr, A. (2017). Common errors in reasoning about the future: Three informal fallacies. *Technological Forecasting and Social Change, 116*, 322–330.

El Naqa, I., & Murphy, M. J. (2015). What is machine learning? In *Machine learning in radiation oncology* (pp. 3–11). Springer.

European Commission. (2022). The Future of Work. https://research-and-innovation.ec.europa.eu/research-area/industry/future-work_en

Figueroa, V. (2018). Data and its impacts on workers and citizens. *Medium.com*, 29 August.

Gartner. (2022). *Future of Work*. Gartner Human Resource Glossary. https://www.gartner.com/en/human-resources/glossary/future-of-work

Goertzel, B., & Pennachin, C. (2007). *Artificial general intelligence* (Vol. 2). Springer.

Hoendervanger, J. G., De Been, I., Van Yperen, N. W., Mobach, M. P., & Albers, C. J. (2016). Flexibility in use: Switching behaviour and satisfaction in activity-based work environments. *Journal of Corporate Real Estate*.

International Labour Organization (ILO). (2017). Inception report for the global commission on the Future of Work.

Kojo, I., & Nenonen, S. (2016). Typologies for co-working spaces in Finland–What and how? *Facilities*.

Kojo, I., & Nenonen, S. (2017). Evolution of co-working places: drivers and possibilities. *Intelligent buildings international, 9*(3), 164–175.

Kolade, O., & Owoseni, A. (2022). Employment 5.0: The work of the future and the Future of Work. *Technology in Society, 102086*.

Lee, M. K., Kusbit, D., Metsky, E., & Dabbish, L. (2015, April). Working with machines: The impact of algorithmic and data-driven management on human workers. In *Proceedings of the 33rd annual ACM conference on human factors in computing systems* (pp. 1603–1612). Association for Computing Machinery.

Lynn, T., Rosati, P., Conway, E., Curran, D., Fox, G., & O'Gorman, C. (2022). *Digital towns: Accelerating and measuring the digital transformation of rural societies and economies* (p. 213). Springer Nature.

Malone, T. W., Rus, D., & Laubacher, R. (2020). Artificial intelligence and the future of work. A report prepared by MIT Task Force on the work of the future. *Research Brief, 17*, 1–39.

Martin, A. (2008). Digital literacy and the "digital society". *Digital Literacies: Concepts, Policies and Practices, 30*(2008), 151–176.

Mateescu, A., & Nguyen, A. (2019). Algorithmic management in the workplace. *Data & Society*, 1–15.

Milgram, P., & Kishino, F. (1994). A taxonomy of mixed reality visual displays. *IEICE Transactions on Information and Systems, 77*(12), 1321–1329.

Mindell, D. A., & Reynolds, E. (2022). *The Work of the Future: Building Better Jobs in an Age of Intelligent Machines*. MIT Press.

Mitchell, R., Shen, Y., & Snell, L. (2022). The future of work: A systematic literature review. *Accounting and Finance, 62*(2), 2667–2686.

Mohamed, M. (2012). Ergonomics of bridge employment. *Work, 41*(Suppl. 1), 307–312.

Oxford English Dictionary. (2022). *Algorithm*. Oxford University Press. https://www.oxfordlearnersdictionaries.com/definition/english/algorithm

Poell, T., Nieborg, D., & Van Dijck, J. (2019). Platformisation. Internet. *Policy Review, 8*(4), 1–13.

Reis, J., Amorim, M., Melão, N., & Matos, P. (2018, March). Digital transformation: A literature review and guidelines for future research. In *World conference on information systems and technologies* (pp. 411–421). Springer.

Rossitto, C., Lampinen, A., & Franzén, C. G. (2017). Hoffice: Social innovation through sustainable nomadic communities. *International Reports on Socio-Informatics (IRSI), 14*(3), 49–55.

Santana, M., & Cobo, M. J. (2020). What is the future of work? A science mapping analysis. *European Management Journal, 38*(6), 846–862.

Schloerb, D. W. (1995). A quantitative measure of telepresence. *Presence Teleoperators and Virtual Environments, 4*(1), 64–80.

Schwartz, J., Hatfield, S., Jones, R., & Anderson, S. (2019). *What is the future of work? Redefining work, workforces, and workplaces.* Deloitte.

Schwellnus, C., Geva, A., & Pak Mathilde, V. R. (2019). *Gig economy platforms: Boon or bane?* Organisation for Economic Co-operation and Development, Economics Department Working Papers, 1550.

Selenko, E., Bankins, S., Shoss, M., Warburton, J., & Restubog, S. L. D. (2022). Artificial intelligence and the Future of Work: A functional-identity perspective. *Current Directions in Psychological Science, 31*(3), 272–279.

Sherman, W. R., & Craig, A. B. (2018). *Understanding virtual reality: Interface, application, and design.* Morgan Kaufmann.

Society for Human Resource Management (SHRM). (2022). What is meant by "the future of work"? https://www.shrm.org/resourcesandtools/tools-and-samples/hr-qa/pages/what-is-meant-by-the-future-of-work.aspx

Stephenson, N. (1992). *Snow crash.* Bantam Books.

Stoepfgeshoff, S. (2018). The Future of Work: Work for the future. *ISM Journal of International Business, 2*(2).

UNCTAD. (2021). *Technology and innovation report 2021.* United Nations Publications. https://unctad.org/page/technology-and-innovation-report-2021

Webster, F. (2006). *Theories of the information society.* Routledge.

Weil, D. (2014). The fissured workplace. In *The fissured workplace.* Harvard University Press.

Willcocks, L. (2020). Robo-Apocalypse cancelled? Reframing the automation and future of work debate. *Journal of Information Technology, 35*(4), 286–302.

World Bank. (2021). Small and Medium Enterprises (SMEs) finance. https://www.worldbank.org/en/topic/smefinance

World Economic Forum. (2018). *The future of jobs report.* World Economic Forum.

CHAPTER 2

Assessing the Impact of New Ways of Working on Individual and Organisational Well-Being

Kathy Monks, Yseult Freeney, and Edel Conway

Abstract This chapter uses self-determination theory (SDT) as an organising framework to consider the impact of new ways of working (NWW) on employee well-being. We focus on the universal needs at the centre of SDT, namely autonomy, competence and relatedness, and explore how each has been impacted by NWW and the ramifications for employees' well-being. Our chapter concludes with a framework encapsulating enablers and inhibitors of employee well-being in the context of NWW.

Keywords Self-determination theory (SDT) • Autonomy • Competence • Relatedness • New ways of working (NWW)

K. Monks • Y. Freeney • E. Conway (✉)
DCU Business School, Dublin City University, Dublin, Ireland
e-mail: kathy.monks@dcu.ie; yseult.freeney@dcu.ie; edel.conway@dcu.ie

T. Lynn et al. (eds.), *The Future of Work*, Palgrave Studies in Digital Business & Enabling Technologies,
https://doi.org/10.1007/978-3-031-31494-0_2

2.1 Introduction

New ways of working (NWW) encompass work practices that include "teleworking, nomadic working, hot-desking, working at co-working spaces, virtual working or mobile working" that are enabled by "complex information systems and virtualised organisational formations (e.g., network enterprises or internet platforms)" (Aroles et al., 2021, p. 1). In consultancy terms, NWW are often referred to as "bricks, bytes, and behaviour changes", involving the integrated management of spatiotemporal, technological and organisational cultural changes (Kingma, 2019). NWW extend the notion of work away from traditional organisational structures and permanent employment to include, for example, crowdwork and online labour platforms (Howcroft & Bergvall-Kåreborn, 2019). NWW are also characterised by both temporal and spatial flexibility. For temporal flexibility, employers may introduce flexibility in working hours to meet customer or employee demands (Spreitzer et al., 2017). Spatial flexibility ranges from situations where employees work at home or another location one or more days each week to those where employees work remotely all the time and may even work in a different geographic location to that of their employing organisation. New spatial working arrangements, such as coworking spaces, makerspaces, hackerspaces and fablabs (Brakel-Ahmed et al., 2020), have also emerged. These working arrangements are enabled by the extensive use of mobile and network information technologies such as the internet, smartphones and cloud computing, together with applications, such as Zoom and Microsoft Teams, that enable individuals to meet in virtual spaces. In addition, firms are increasingly relying on digital technologies to configure the way in which work is accomplished with performance now increasingly monitored through advances in algorithmic management[1] (Parent-Rocheleau & Parker, 2021; Wang et al., 2020).

This chapter focuses on aspects of NWW that appear to have the most impact on employee well-being. Grant et al. (2007, p. 52) define work-related well-being as "the overall quality of an employee's experience and functioning at work" and suggest it comprises three main facets: psychological, physical and social functioning. We use self-determination theory (SDT) as an organising framework through which to explore NWW and well-being. SDT encompasses a focus on both intrinsic and extrinsic sources of motivation that impact both cognitive and social development

[1] See Chap. 4 for a more detailed discussion.

at work, including factors that facilitate or undermine people's sense of well-being and their performance (Deci & Ryan, 2012). We examine the universal needs at the centre of SDT, namely autonomy, competence and relatedness, and consider how they may mediate the impact of NWW on employee well-being. We then present a model which identifies the main enablers and inhibitors of well-being in the context of NWW. In conclusion, we examine how the Covid-19 pandemic has imposed NWW in an unanticipated way on very large numbers of employees (Kniffin et al., 2021) and the implications for both individual and organisational well-being.

2.2 New Ways of Working and Autonomy

Autonomy is a core concept in SDT where it is viewed as a basic psychological need defined as self-governance or rule by the self and identified as crucial to well-being (Ryan & Deci, 2000). Studies that have explored the relationship between autonomy and NWW present conflicting evidence of its impact on employee well-being. For example, remote gig workers managed through algorithmic management processes report high levels of autonomy, task variety and complexity, but they may have little choice except to work from home and to work unsociable hours to meet client demands. As a result, they experience feelings of social isolation, overwork, sleep deprivation and exhaustion, all of which have a negative impact on well-being (Wood et al., 2018).

Another study of knowledge workers (Spivack & Woodside, 2019) indicated that autonomy in choice of work location was associated with different outcomes depending on a wide range of individual-level factors including gender, age, levels of intrinsic motivation, and family and home circumstances. In this study of academics in a university in the USA, perceptions of work location autonomy were also dependent on whether academics perceived they benefitted from higher productivity and/or well-being outcomes. A recent study showed that the provision of flexible working practices increased trust in management, leading to a decrease in job-related anxiety. Job autonomy moderated the relationship between flexible working practices and trust in management, with this relationship being stronger when perceived autonomy was high (Yunus & Mostafa, 2021).

A variety of negative well-being outcomes including stress, burnout, exhaustion and increased workload (Karimikia et al., 2021) have been linked to the extensive use of Information and Communications Technology (ICT) which is core to NWW. Again, the evidence is complex in regard to the relationship between employee autonomy, ICT use and employee well-being. Some studies have shown that autonomy mitigates the impact of ICT use on negative employee outcomes (e.g., Chelsey, 2014), but a recent meta-analytic review (Karimikia et al., 2021) found that high levels of autonomy among employees exacerbated work stress among employees using ICT.

Explanations for this finding lie in the ways in which ICT systems are designed. Such systems may enforce a particular way of working or decision-making which is at odds with the methods that employees with high levels of autonomy prefer. As the technological capability of ICT systems increases, they may more frequently be used to monitor and control employee performance. When this occurs, ICT systems may emphasise aspects of work that can be quantified, rather than the perhaps more interesting or meaningful aspects of the job (Schafheitle et al., 2020). This focus may restrict choices that employees make in the methods they use or the tasks they undertake, particularly where those tasks are rewarded financially, with a negative impact on autonomy (Parent-Rocheleau & Parker, 2021). ICT use may also invade autonomy in personal lives. The boundaries between work and non-work may blur as ICT has a pervasive capacity to invade personal time and space so that employees find themselves working outside their normal working hours, thus reducing autonomy in their personal lives, with negative effects on their well-being, including work-family conflict, emotional exhaustion and poor sleep quality (e.g., Wang et al., 2020).

Given this evidence, it is perhaps not surprising that the term "autonomy paradox" (Mazmanian et al., 2013) is used to describe how, in situations of remote working, professionals' reliance on mobile devices both increases and diminishes their autonomy. These devices provide flexibility and control in the short-term, but simultaneously intensify professionals' availability to management, thus reducing their ability to disconnect from work. This notion of paradox can also be applied to flexible working arrangements more generally, with flexible working understood as fluctuating and constantly being shaped. To retain and enhance autonomy and well-being in NWW, organisations need to ensure that both they and their employees respect the boundaries between work and non-work, thus ensuring that employees retain control over their non-work lives and avoid problems with work-home conflict. Measures include ensuring that emails or phone calls are not sent or answered outside standard working hours. Organisations also need to invest in learning and development so that employees are equipped to make informed choices over the methods they use in undertaking work tasks.

2.3 New Ways of Working and Competence

Within SDT, competence involves the experience of mastery and being effective in one's activities (Ryan & Deci, 2000). Satisfying the three universal needs has been found to support work motivation and well-being (Van den Broeck et al., 2016), but there is some evidence that satisfying the need for competence may be the most important in the triad for supporting employee well-being. For instance, in research undertaken during the Covid-19 pandemic among people mandated to work remotely, competence was most strongly predictive of well-being over autonomy and relatedness (Cantarero et al., 2021). When individuals do not feel capable and effective, they can not only feel demotivated, but their well-being is also seriously at risk (Deci & Ryan, 2012). The interactions between individuals and their environments provide them with feedback through the completion of tasks—but there is also a significant relational element to feedback that may be hampered in NWW designs.

There are numerous ways in which NWW pose a risk to fulfilment of the need for competence that are rooted in relational dimensions of the workplace, where remote employees are cut off from the naturally occurring, formal and informal relationships that form a key dimension of their work. The risk to competence is not inevitable, but, without careful planning and deliberate attempts to mitigate it, employees could find their need for competence thwarted. SDT research points to feedback as a critical driver of competence. In a major meta-analytical study, positive feedback was found to enhance intrinsic motivation (Deci et al., 1999), while other research has linked meaningful feedback that highlights an individual's mastery of a task to a sense of competence (Hagger et al., 2015). Deci (1971) also emphasised the role of unexpected positive encouragement and feedback in driving intrinsic motivation and well-being. This type of feedback helps people to feel more competent, which is one of the key needs for personal growth. In fully remote working contexts, workers can be cut off from this valuable informal feedback. In the case of remote workers and particularly gig workers, there will be less access to infrastructural supports, such as career mentors or role models and diminished networking, career and skill development opportunities (Ashford et al., 2018), all critical to the development of work-related skills and knowledge sharing.

Drawing on both SDT and social cognitive theory, we know that individuals derive a sense of competence through their informal interactions with—and observations of—others. Competence relies heavily on social benchmarks in the workplace and valuable learning occurs through the observation of others' successes and failures (Bledow et al., 2017). Role modelling, social comparison and vicarious experience are relational drivers of competence (Manz & Sims Jr, 1981), all of which are less accessible to individuals who work remotely. Coworking and hybrid options at least offer some opportunity for an individual to access relevant social comparatives that can support competence through access to informal learning, peer observation and "mentoring in the moment" (Johnson & Smith, 2019).

Finally, when considering competence satisfaction in NWW models, it would be remiss to overlook the roles of both digital and trust competency in reducing the potential negative impact on overall competence because of greater relational isolation. In their Digital Resilience Competency Framework, Grant and Clarke (2020) identify factors that support positive remote working experiences that promote rather than inhibit employee well-being, productivity and engagement. They identify key requirements including digital skills, trust-building skills, self-care skills, and social and emotional skills.

This points to several ways by which competency needs can be met in NWW. First, digital competency was found to protect workers who worked remotely during the Covid-19 pandemic. Individual competencies related to technology allow employees to be more productive and less stressed under remote working conditions (Tramontano et al., 2021). Second, being able to self-regulate and manage one's time, working independently as well as coping with disruptions, also support performance and well-being in remote contexts (Grant et al., 2013). Finally, relational skills are key to navigating remote working and protecting a sense of competence. In particular, trust competency refers to the ability of individuals to build trusting relationships at work (Tramontano et al., 2021). One challenge to effective remote work is the inability of managers to trust employees to get on with the job (Kniffin et al., 2021), and this lack of trust can risk employees feeling less competent. Being able to build trust across digital platforms will enhance competence while the most 'well-adjusted remote workers' in Tramontano et al.'s (2021) study, who reported high levels of engagement and productivity, were characterised by high levels of trust skills.

2.4 New Ways of Working and Relatedness

Relatedness refers to an individual's need to seek out mutual and meaningful connections and to experience a sense of community or a belongingness with others (Deci & Ryan, 2000). Loneliness, on the other hand, is "the psychological pain of perceived relational deficiencies in the workplace" (Wright & Silard, 2021, p. 1074). The experience of belonginess or loneliness may vary according to individual differences; at one extreme *sociotropy* represents an excessive desire for close interpersonal relationships and social attention, while at the other extreme, *social anhedonia* represents a marked disinterest in such relationships and attention (Wright & Silard, 2021). Social anhedonics are unlikely to experience loneliness at work because their desire for social relationships is minimal. However, individuals at the sociotropic extreme are susceptible to loneliness because their needs and expectations for relatedness at work may be excessively high. Deci and Ryan (2000, p. 71) point out that while "proximal relational supports may not be necessary for intrinsic motivation; a secure relational base does seem important". High levels of relatedness exist in work environments characterised by genuine interest, care and friendship amongst employees (Slemp et al., 2021; Van den Broeck et al., 2016). Research suggests that even routine workplace conversations, such as informal chats and "watercooler moments", can be critical in creating a sense of community and enhancing both mental and physical well-being (Mogilner et al., 2018). Walton et al.'s (2012) experimental research also suggests that *mere belonging* (i.e., even minimal cues of social connection) can lead people to develop shared goals and motivations.

Van den Broeck et al. (2016, p. 1199) suggest that the need for relatedness is "less immediately essential for some outcomes than the needs for autonomy and competence". For example, some people may enjoy working alone, meaning that the work itself may not satisfy their need for relatedness. Some studies suggest that professionals who engage in complex tasks requiring little interaction are happier and more productive when working remotely (Allen et al., 2014). Other evidence suggests that remote working can lead to small and positive impacts on work-life balance and employee well-being for those working remotely for less than 2.5

days per week, but anything beyond that can be harmful to workplace relationships (Gajendran & Harrison, 2007). Consistent with this view, it is suggested that a greater reliance on technology at work can lead to loneliness and burnout (Moss, 2018), particularly when individuals are working remotely (Charalampous et al., 2019; Wang et al., 2021). In a recent study on virtual working during the Covid-19 pandemic, Wang et al. (2021) identified a number of virtual work characteristics that were linked to workers' performance and well-being via challenges including loneliness. They found that social support was linked to fewer challenges during remote working and that job autonomy in particular was negatively related to loneliness. Further evidence suggests that remote workers may experience barriers to communication leading to them feeling 'out of the loop' because they do not see how their work fits with their wider team's or organisation's goals (Gajendran & Harrison, 2007).

One of the characteristics of work in the gig economy is that it is often carried out alone, where gig workers feel like "perpetual strangers" to other similar workers or to the clients of their work (Kunda et al., 2002, p. 250). To meet their need for relatedness, many remote and gig workers work in publicly accessible spaces such as coffee shops or public libraries, which can lack privacy and offer limited opportunities for social engagement. The emergence and growth of coworking spaces in recent years has given rise to an alternative work setting that creates a more relational work setting (e.g., community, social networks), as well as infrastructural supports (e.g., Wi-Fi, IT security) (Garrett et al., 2017). Evidence suggests that workers opt to engage in coworking not so much for the space, but because it offers a greater sense of community and creates a social experience that corresponds to their need to belong (Garrett et al., 2017). Having such a sense of community has been associated with increased psychological health and well-being (e.g., Prezza & Costantini, 1998).

To encourage a greater sense of relatedness in NWW, managers and organisations will need to engage in more supportive management practices by communicating with workers using motivational language, showing a genuine concern for workers' well-being, building trust among distributed teams and sharing information (Wang et al., 2021). In addition, remote workers should engage in informal communication with other colleagues, including use of work-related social networking platforms (e.g., Slack), to socialise informally to enhance their job satisfaction and to reduce loneliness. Given the relational constraints faced by gig workers, Ashford et al. (2018) suggest the need for such workers to craft a relational support system that will provide a buffer against the stressors and strains of gig work and to develop relational agility—that is an ability to form, maintain and discontinue relationships productively. They suggest that these supports will not only enable gig workers to survive but will allow them to positively thrive in their work.

2.5 Managing New Ways of Working Using a Self-determination Perspective

Our chapter has examined the impact of NWW on individual and organisational well-being. Using SDT as our organising framework has highlighted the relationships and interdependencies between autonomy, competence and relatedness in shaping the work experiences of employees engaged in NWW. Contrary to the view that relatedness is less essential for work outcomes (Van den Broeck et al., 2016), our review suggests that it is set to become an important bedrock that will support the needs for autonomy and competence in the new world of work. Figure 2.1

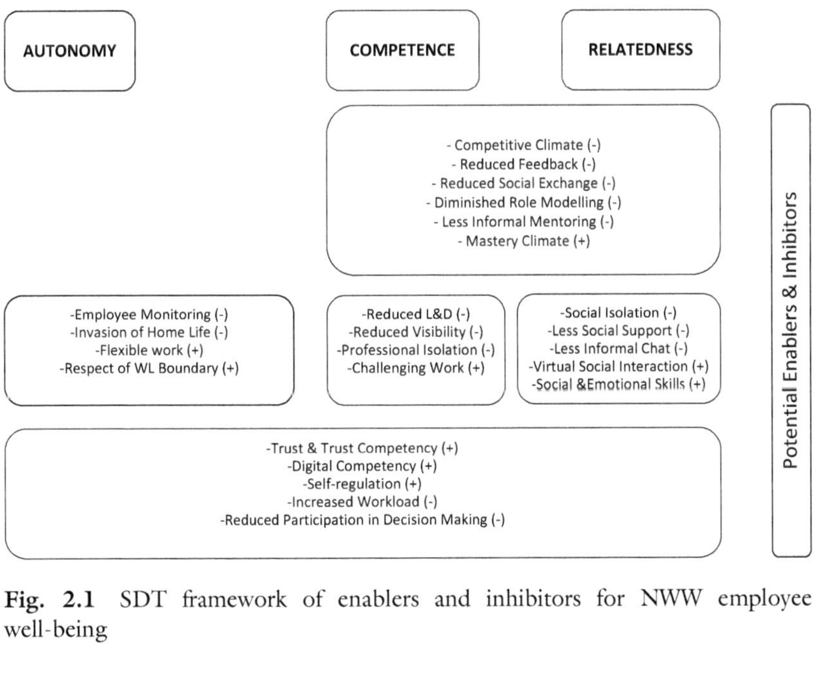

Fig. 2.1 SDT framework of enablers and inhibitors for NWW employee well-being

summarises the main enablers and inhibitors of well-being using the SDT framework and indicates the ways in which organisations can enhance well-being in NWW via the autonomy, competence and relatedness dimensions that underpin SDT.

We propose that the development of competence and relatedness will be more likely in organisations with a mastery rather than a performance culture (Wright & Silard, 2021). This is because such environments will support cooperation, knowledge sharing and learning, unlike performance cultures which will emphasise competition and social comparison. Our model highlights the complementarities that exist across all three dimensions, signalling the potential for these practices to have powerful synergies to maximise well-being.

2.6 Conclusion

Our chapter has highlighted the complexity of understanding the impact of NWW on well-being, a complexity heightened by the impact of Covid-19. The rapid transformation in work practices that accompanied Covid-19 was made possible by the increased digitisation and automation of workplaces and the widespread adoption of machine learning, data analytics and robotics (Nigel, 2020). For many workers this has led to a deterioration in working conditions with an intensification of work, increased monitoring, control and job insecurity (Hoddar, 2020). At the same time, there is evidence of workers responding to these challenges. For some, this means quitting their jobs and exploring more meaningful work options, resulting in labour shortages for many firms (Aroles et al., 2021). Others are engaging with NWW, for example through coworking arrangements, to enhance self-determination through "spatial self-management" (Endrissat & Leclercq-Vandelannoitte, 2021). In whatever ways technology is used to shape the continued emergence of NWW, there will be a need to integrate supports for autonomy, competence and relatedness if employee well-being is to be sustained.

References

Allen, T. D., Cho, E., & Meier, L. L. (2014). Work–family boundary dynamics. *Annual Review of Organizational Psychology and Organizational Behaviour, 1*(1), 99–121.

Aroles, J., Cecez-Kecmanovic, D., Dale, K., Kingma, S., & Mitev, N. (2021). New Ways of Working (NWW): Workplace transformation in the digital age. *Information and Organization, 31*(4), 1–11.

Ashford, S. J., Caza, B. B., & Reid, E. M. (2018). From surviving to thriving in the gig economy: A research agenda for individuals in the new world of work. *Research in Organizational Behavior, 38*, 23–41.

Bledow, R., Carette, B., Kühnel, J., & Bister, D. (2017). Learning from others' failures: The effectiveness of failure stories for managerial learning. *Academy of Management Learning & Education, 16*(1), 39–53.

Brakel-Ahmed, F., Cnossen, B., & Schlegelmilch, J. (2020). Discovering workspaces: Towards a typology of collective workspaces. In F. Mntanari, E. Mattarelli, & A. C. Scapolan (Eds.), *Collaborative spaces at work: Innovation, creativity and relations* (pp. 37–49). Routledge.

Cantarero, K., van Tilburg, W. A., & Smoktunowicz, E. (2021). Affirming basic psychological needs promotes mental well-being during the COVID-19 outbreak. *Social Psychological and Personality Science, 12*(5), 821–828.

Charalampous, M., Grant, C. A., Tramontano, C., & Michailidis, E. (2019). Systematically reviewing remote e-workers' well-being at work: A multidimensional approach. *European Journal of Work and Organizational Psychology, 28*(1), 51–73.

Chelsey, N. (2014). Information and communication technology use, work intensification and employee stress and distress. *Work, Employment and Society, 28*(4), 589–610.

Deci, E. L. (1971). Effects of externally mediated rewards on intrinsic motivation. *Journal of Personality and Social Psychology, 18*(1), 105.

Deci, E. L., Koestner, R., & Ryan, R. M. (1999). A meta-analytic review of experiments examining the effects of extrinsic rewards on intrinsic motivation. *Psychological Bulletin, 125*(6), 627.

Deci, E. L., & Ryan, R. M. (2000). The 'what' and 'why' of goal pursuits: Human needs and the self-determination of behavior. *Psychological Inquiry, 11*, 227–268.

Deci, E. L., & Ryan, R. M. (2012). Self-determination theory. In P. A. M. Van Lange, A. W. Kruglanski, & E. T. Higgins (Eds.), *Handbook of theories of social psychology* (Vol. 1, pp. 416–437). Sage.

Endrissat, N., & Leclercq-Vandelannoitte, A. (2021). From sites to vibes: Technology and the spatial production of coworking spaces. *Information and Organization, 31*. https://doi.org/10.1016/j.infoandorg.2021.100353

Gajendran, R. S., & Harrison, D. A. (2007). The good, the bad, and the unknown about telecommuting: Meta-analysis of psychological mediators and individual consequences. *Journal of Applied Psychology, 92*(6), 1524–1541.

Garrett, L. E., Spreitzer, G. M., & Bacevice, P. A. (2017). Co-constructing a sense of community at work: The emergence of community in coworking spaces. *Organization Studies, 38*(6), 821–842.

Grant, A., Christianson, M., & Price, R. (2007). Happiness, health or relationships? Managerial practices and employee well-being trade-offs. *Academy of Management Executive, 21*(1), 51–63.

Grant, C., & Clarke, C. (2020). Digital resilience: A competency framework for agile workers. In *Agile working and well-being in the digital age* (pp. 117–130). Palgrave Macmillan.

Grant, C. A., Wallace, L. M., & Spurgeon, P. C. (2013). An exploration of the psychological factors affecting remote e-worker's job effectiveness, well-being and work-life balance. *Employee Relations, 35*, 527–546.

Hagger, M. S., Koch, S., & Chatzisarantis, N. L. (2015). The effect of causality orientations and positive competence-enhancing feedback on intrinsic motivation: A test of additive and interactive effects. *Personality and Individual Differences, 72*, 107–111.

Hoddar, A. (2020). New technology, work and employment in the era of COVID-19: Reflecting on legacies of research. *New Technology, Work and Employment, 35*, 262–275.

Howcroft, D., & Bergvall-Kåreborn, B. (2019). A typology of crowdwork platforms. *Work, Employment and Society, 33*, 21–38.

Johnson, B., & Smith, D. G. (2019). Real mentorship starts with company culture, not formal programs. *Harvard Business Review*. Retrieved October 28, 2021, from https://hbr.org/2019/12/real-mentorship-starts-with-company-culture-not-formal-programs

Karimikia, H., Singh, H., & Joseph, D. (2021). Negative outcomes of ICT use at work: Meta-analytic evidence and the role of job autonomy. *Internet Research, 31*(1), 159–190. https://doi.org/10.1108/INTR-09-2019-0385

Kingma, S. (2019). New Ways of Working (NWW): Work space and cultural change in virtualizing organizations. *Culture and Organization, 25*(5), 383–406.

Kniffin, K. M., et al. (2021). COVID-19 and the workplace: Implications, issues, and insights for future research and action. *American Psychologist, 76*(1), 63–77.

Kunda, G., Barley, S. R., & Evans, J. (2002). Why do contractors contract? The experience of highly skilled technical professionals in a contingent labour market. *Industrial and Labor Relations Review, 55*(2), 234–261.

Manz, C. C., & Sims, H. P., Jr. (1981). Vicarious learning: The influence of modeling on organizational behavior. *Academy of Management Review, 6*(1), 105–113.

Mazmanian, M., Orlikowski, W., & Yates, J. (2013). The autonomy paradox: The implications of mobile email devices for knowledge professionals. *Organization Science, 24*(5), 1337–1357.

Mogilner, C., Whillans, A., & Norton, M. I. (2018). Time, money, and subjective wellbeing. In E. Diener, S. Oishi, & L. Tay (Eds.), *Handbook of well-being* (Noba Scholar handbook series: Subjective well-being). DEF Publishers.

Moss, J. (2018). Helping remote workers avoid loneliness and burnout. *Harvard Business Review on Health*.

Nigel, L. (2020). The influence of the COVID-19 on the digital transformation of work. *International Journal of Sociology and Social Policy, 40*, 861–865.

Parent-Rocheleau, X., & Parker, S. (2021). Algorithms as work designers: How algorithmic management influences the design of jobs. *Human Resource Management Review*. https://doi.org/10.1016/j.hrmr2021.100838

Prezza, M., & Costantini, S. (1998). Sense of community and life satisfaction: Investigation in three different territorial contexts. *Journal of Community & Applied Social Psychology, 8*, 181–194.

Ryan, R. M., & Deci, E. L. (2000). Self-determination theory and the facilitation of intrinsic motivation, social development, and well-being. *American Psychologist, 55*(1), 68.

Schafheitle, S. D., Weibel, A., Ebert, I. L., Kasper, G., Schank, C., & Leicht-Deobald, U. (2020). No stone left unturned? Towards a framework for the impact of datafication technologies on organizational control. *Academy of Management Discoveries, 6*(3), 455–487.

Slemp, G., Lee, M. A., & Mossman, L. H. (2021). Interventions to support autonomy, competence, and relatedness needs in organizations: A systematic review with recommendations for research and practice. *Journal of Occupational and Organizational Psychology, 94*(2), 427–457.

Spivack, A., & Woodside, A. (2019). Applying complexity theory for modelling human resource outcomes: Antecedent configurations indicating perceived location autonomy and work environment choice. *Journal of Business Research, 102*, 109–119.

Spreitzer, G., Cameron, L., & Garrett, L. (2017). Alternative work arrangements: Two images of the new world of work. *Annual Review of Organizational Psychology and Organizational Behaviour, 4*, 473–499.

Tramontano, C., Grant, C., & Clarke, C. (2021). Development and validation of the e-work self-efficacy scale to assess digital competencies in remote working. *Computers in Human Behavior Reports, 4*, 100129.

Van den Broeck, A., Ferris, D. L., Chang, C. H., & Rosen, C. C. (2016). A review of self-determination theory's basic psychological needs at work. *Journal of Management, 42*, 1195–1229.

Walton, G. M., Cohen, G. L., Cwir, D., & Spencer, S. J. (2012). Mere belonging: The power of social connections. *Journal of Personality and Social Psychology, 102*(3), 513–532.

Wang, B., Liu, Y., & Parker, S. (2020). How does the use of information communication technology affect individuals? A work design perspective. *Academy of Management Annals, 14*(2), 695–725.

Wang, B., Liu, Y., Qian, J., & Parker, S. K. (2021). Achieving effective remote working during the COVID-19 pandemic: A work design perspective. *Applied Psychology, 70*(1), 16–59.

Wood, A., Graham, V., & Lehdonvirta, V. (2018). Good gig bad gig: Autonomy and algorithmic control in the global gig economy. *Work, Employment and Society, 33*(1), 56–75.

Wright, S., & Silard, A. (2021). Unravelling the antecedents of loneliness in the workplace. *Human Relations, 74*(7), 1060–1081.

Yunus, S., & Mostafa, A. (2021). Flexible working practices and job-related anxiety: Examining the roles of trust in management and job autonomy. *Economic and Industrial Democracy*. https://doi.org/10.1177/0143831X21995259

CHAPTER 3

AI, Data Analytics and the Professions

Brid Murphy and Orla Feeney

Abstract Advances in artificial intelligence (AI) and data analytics are having a transformative effect on how work is performed. Research suggests that such technologies will wholly displace some professions while fundamentally changing where professionals expend time and effort in their day-to-day roles. The legal and accounting professions in particular are being transformed by AI and data analytics. This chapter discusses the nature of professions, the shift in use of AI and data analytics from process-oriented activities to knowledge-oriented activities, and how the legal and accounting professions are responding.

Keywords Professions • Artificial intelligence • Data analytics

B. Murphy (✉) • O. Feeney
DCU Business School, Dublin City University, Dublin, Ireland
e-mail: brid.murphy@dcu.ie; orla.feeney@dcu.ie

T. Lynn et al. (eds.), *The Future of Work*, Palgrave Studies in Digital Business & Enabling Technologies,
https://doi.org/10.1007/978-3-031-31494-0_3

3.1 Introduction

Much has been written in recent years about the threat posed by technology to traditional professional roles, with some alarming assertions that many professional roles are set to be replaced by a dizzying array of digital technologies. The reality is much more nuanced. Indeed, many aspects of the work of professionals will be subject to major change in the coming years in keeping with the broader digital transformation of society. We can be certain that these developments, incorporating technological innovations and new ways of working, will have a profound effect on the institutional arrangements and social processes of those working within the professions. This chapter explores how communities of organisations within the field of professional services, and specifically lawyers and accountants, are responding to the changes posed by the proliferation of digital technology. Following a discussion on the nature of 'professions' and how they have evolved in response to economic, technological and social changes, we discuss how artificial intelligence (AI) and data analytics are impacting two professions, law and accounting. This provides a basis for re-imagining the Future of Work in the professions in the context of current and future challenges.

3.2 Professions: An Overview

It is broadly accepted that modern *professions* are recognised as organised groups of individuals who do different things (task differentiation or specialisation), in different workplaces, for different clients (client differentiation). Professional practices may be understood as "embodied, materially mediated arrays of human activity centrally organised around shared practical understanding" (Schatzki, 2001, p. 2). In turn, Professionalism is more difficult to describe but should not be perceived simply as "the software that goes with the hardware of an actual profession" (Burns, 2019, p. 50). *Professionalism* focuses on the conduct, qualities and behaviours that characterise a profession. It acknowledges that professional practitioners often find themselves in ambiguous, ill-defined, unprecedented situations for which existing theories and models of practice may not immediately guide them and where significant judgement is required (Schon, 1983).

To appropriately understand the impact of current technological challenges, it is first necessary to examine the characteristics of professions.

Professions may be described as occupational groupings organised around an identifiable proprietary corpus of theoretical or abstract knowledge or technique. The work professionals do is "esoteric, complex and discretionary in character" (Freidson, 1994, p. 200), focused on the provision of customised, knowledge-based services to a client base, where the professionals maintain control over client selection. Professional association enhances the status, authority and credibility of members and the collective professions. Without this association, the designation is devalued and the purpose of having a professional status is defeated (Eraut, 1994). Extensive levels of individual autonomy are prevalent within professional practice, coupled with relatively low levels of managerial authority and intervention (Empson et al., 2015). This involves judgement, reflexivity, flexibility and creativity in the application of the specialist corpus of knowledge (Blomgren & Waks, 2015). Individual professionals are also deemed capable of self-regulation, controlling themselves by co-operative, collective means. Professions and professionals exhibit a shared concrete and unique culture, which incorporates a rhetoric involving a series of values, norms, meanings, symbols, attitudes, perspectives and behaviours common to members of the particular profession (Brock et al., 2014). Hager and Hodkinson (2011) discuss the concept of a tacit ladder, where novices may ultimately progress from lower rungs to become accomplished expert professionals at the top, through immersion into established and skilful participation within a community of practice.

Research by the World Economic Forum (WEF) (2018, 2020) suggests that clusters within professions will be wholly displaced and others will spend increased time "on tasks related to communicating and interacting" rather than on tasks that were previously conceived as core information-generating tasks (WEF, 2018, p. 15). The overall viability of some professions is currently under threat: two such professions highlighted are law and accounting. The recent democratisation of information and knowledge has led to some non-law businesses offering legal services. The profession's chief response to date has been to deconstruct its tasks and to engage non-professionals, for example paralegals, who have a lower cost base to complete more routine tasks or to outsource to offshore lower costs providers (Susskind, 2013). Similarly, as technology has facilitated the distribution of accounting information allowing non-specialists to complete accounting tasks, some have suggested that further technological developments might lead to accountant roles becoming entirely redundant (Frey & Osborne, 2017). Yet, we have seen an increase in accounting roles, with accounting professionals spending more time interpreting and communicating rather than preparing a growing volume of data. This trend however masks the fact that many accounting professionals have had to augment their training and transition to new roles (Bessen, 2018).

It is clear that technological advances have forced re-examination of the production, supply and "servicification" of professional expertise (Baldwin, 2016). The traditional template of professions is progressively unbundling and reforming in new ways (Boussard, 2018). Such changes will propel professions to change more radically than ever before as they respond to the challenges posed by technological innovations (Susskind, 2021; Susskind & Susskind, 2015).

3.3 The Enduring Technological Revolution

IBM's first mainframe computer in 1952 signalled the beginning of technological advances which have impacted all of society. Roles and functions across almost all areas of the workforce have adapted in response to each stage of technological advancement (Bessen, 2018). However, the velocity of these developments has increased exponentially and the escalating fusion of technologies has become a key driver of change in professional roles and practices. AI and data analytics have particularly captured the attention of academics and practitioners in the past two decades. Both legal and accounting professionals increasingly seek to harness their potential in order to enhance the value of their professional contribution. Other technologies have, of course, affected aspects of work within the fields of law and accounting. For example, blockchain has the capacity to democratise access to legal services through smart contracts and robotic process automation (RPA) has automated many of the repetitive transaction process-oriented tasks traditionally carried out by humans (Cooper et al., 2019). However, it is AI and analytics which are having a profound impact on each of these professions.

3.3.1 Artificial Intelligence

AI is a vast field encompassing the systemising of activities traditionally associated with human intelligence such as planning, learning, reasoning, logic, problem solving, knowledge representation, perception, manipulation, and even social intelligence and creativity (Frey & Osborne, 2017). Russell and Norvig (2010) distil the various definitions of AI into four

Systems that think like humans	**Systems that think rationally**
For example, how to automate activities traditionally associated with human thinking such as decision-making, problem solving, learning (Bellman 1978)	*For example, how to use computational models to make it possible to perceive, reason and act (Winston 1992)*
Systems that act like humans	**Systems that act rationally**
For example, how to make computers do things which, at the moment, people are better at (Rich and Knight 1991)	*For example, how to design intelligent agents (Poole et al 1998)*

Fig. 3.1 Goals of artificial intelligence (adapted from Russell & Norvig, 2010)

categories which really represent the key goals of AI, as depicted in Fig. 3.1.

AI applications in the top two boxes are concerned with thought process and reasoning while those in the bottom boxes address behaviour. AI applications on the left seek to emulate human performance while those on the right endeavour to produce ideal outcomes. The difference between human (on the left) and rational (on the right) in Russell and Norvig's (2010) typology is really a distinction between imperfect and perfect. AI applications in the left boxes are simply seeking to do things as well as humans can do, using natural language processing, knowledge representation, automated reasoning and machine learning. These AI aspects resonate with the professional—how applications using machine learning, deep learning and data mining can be used to solve the kinds of problems traditionally solved by humans, and moreover, how they improve themselves each time they solve a problem. Early versions of AI concentrated on *simulating* human intelligence, focusing on one task at a time. It was predicated on the prescriptive programming of specific inputs and was incapable of "thinking" beyond specific processing. Machine learning marked the start of significant progress in *replicating* human intelligence, allowing machines to automatically learn from past data without the need to be explicitly programmed. These systems learn to do their jobs and advance based on experience, much like a human professional.

3.3.2 Data Analytics

Data is a corporate asset (Brown et al., 2011) and effective management and analytics of data has become critical to establishing and maintaining competitive advantage (Bughin et al., 2011). Data analytics presents opportunities to access increasing volumes of new information from a variety of sources. The term "small data" refers to data which are small enough in terms of volume to be readily accessible and comprehensible for human comprehension while the shift towards "big data" reflects the voluminous information flows emerging from today's data-driven society. Arguably, analytics itself has not changed significantly—statistics, regression, classification models and hypothesis testing have been around for decades. What has changed is the exponential growth in available data together with a huge increase in computing power available to process it (Liebowitz, 2020). Many organisations have expanded the scope of their information systems from traditional internal data processing to automated data capture connecting businesses to suppliers, affiliates, consumers and clients on a real-time basis. The much expanded availability of data is propelling companies to use large-scale analytics to make decisions (Merendino et al., 2018), innovate (Wu et al., 2020) and navigate crises (Henke et al., 2020). If they are to retain their privileged professional position, lawyers and accountants must navigate this expanded data ecosystem, requiring them to bridge the gap between themselves and the IT department, specifically, the data scientist, the emerging custodian of the growing wealth of organisational data.

The ability of AI and machine learning to automate work, combined with the growing prevalence of big data and the use of smart big data analytics, elevates the true potential of digital technology to replace human endeavour (Loebbecke & Picot, 2015). Together, they are already eroding aspects of professional work and changing the nature and content of professional jobs, through both automation and innovation.

3.4 The Impact of AI and Data Analytics on the Legal and Accounting Professions

Technology was initially utilised in process-oriented activities, but its growing prevalence in the knowledge sector is forcing professionals to rethink how they engage with their roles (Chiu et al., 2016). The extent of the impact of some technological advances and their associated implications for the two highlighted professions—legal and accounting—is now examined.

3.4.1 Legal Profession

Many large clients are challenging the status quo of large legal firms, establishing their own inhouse legal departments or selecting alternative providers, including Big 4 professional services firms who provide multidisciplinary services. These providers are evolving at a pace faster than many law firms and placing an increasing reliance on technology to provide a more efficient and cheaper service, core considerations for many consumers of legal services. In addition, the law is, in some instances, being operated by individual lay consumers. These alternative operations are often based on analyses of big data repositories of publicly available legal provisions and precedents, most of which can be accessed online at no or little cost. They allow the efficient handling of unstructured legal information and the situating of legal issues in the context of pertinent precedent (Alarie et al., 2017). These include Docracy and Neolata Logic which comprise open collections of legal agreements and Westlaw, a database of searchable content including case law, news, legal journals, commentary, current awareness alerts and materials specific to jurisdictions. AI systems are also well established within the legal profession. Expert AI systems which had previously been the domain of legal professionals have now become available to non-specialists, largely operating on a commercial footing. These enable non specialists to examine complex issues and model possible outcomes. International law firm Allen & Overy provides a diagnostic expert system tool which can contend with complex multijurisdictional issues. Elsewhere, CaseCrunch allows users to predict legal decisions based on case precedent. Both of these have outperformed many experienced human legal specialist challengers. Such tools can broaden expertise, empower users and provide greater access to justice and more value to clients (Alarie et al., 2017).

However, the legal profession has proved relatively cautious in adopting technology. This is not wholly unexpected, given the importance of the law to the functioning of society. The pervasiveness of big data and AI capabilities could have serious implications should 'herding' behaviours evidenced in the financial sector prior to the crash of 2008 become the norm within the legal domain (Ayres & Mitts, 2015). Big data systems have a propensity to increasingly rely on "self-reinforcing informational cascades" (Devins et al., 2017, p. 361). Yet, the law is not objectively based on black and white rules or on scientific assumptions. Given that society is constantly evolving and that regulations are continuously being updated in differing spheres, the law too must continuously and substantively evolve. It must remain open to interpretation as its application may vary in different contexts. Suggestions that the law can be a centralised big data repository do not permit this variation or adaptivity. Given their possibilities to replicate human intelligence, it is more difficult to assess the repercussions of reliance on AI tools and techniques. AI is undoubtedly continuing to advance the evolution of the law and the manner in which legal services are provided, by substituting existing processes to change the way legal knowledge is produced and consumed. It remains to be seen whether it may actually revolutionise it (Alarie et al., 2017)—for example lead to personalisation of law i.e. the tailoring of law to individual circumstances.

3.4.2 Accounting Profession

The accounting profession encapsulates a multitude of roles involving the provision of financial-focused information to inform decision-making. These roles fall into two main categories—accountants in business and accountants in practice. Accountants in business have historically embraced change and enhanced their skill sets in response to changes in technology (Bromwich & Bhimani, 1989, 2009). Today, a variety of "off the shelf" software packages are available to smaller organisations with which they can record and report accounting transactions for their businesses—for example Quikbooks, Sage, etc.—while larger entities work with software developers to build customised systems which integrate the various operating components of the organisation—for example SAP, Oracle, etc. Accountants have been dealing with increasing volumes of data for decades. Data analytics simply offers further opportunities in this area. Potential benefits include greater efficiencies around managing datasets, more sophisticated exception reporting in relation to controls and risks, and improved decision-making resulting from enhanced predictive modelling (ICAEW, 2014). Big data also provides a host of opportunities for accountants in practice. Firms are increasingly investing in audit-related technology, which is a game changer in terms of how audits of the future will be conducted. The capacity of data analytics facilitates auditor assessment of entire populations of transactions, effectively putting an end to sampling and the audit risk associated with it (Earley, 2015).

AI knowledge-based systems have been used in accounting since the 1990s. The pattern recognition ability of data mining combined with the predictive power of machine learning is used in cost estimation, forecasting, pricing and financial analysis (Karaca, 2021; Nielsen, 2020; Pakšiová & Oriskóová, 2020). AI systems are used by accountants in practice to enhance judgement accuracy. Key benefits include the reduction of over-auditing, improved management of audit risk and achieving more accurate audit conclusions more quickly (Brazel & Agoglia, 2007). In this way, AI applications may lead to enhanced trust in the audit process (Alles & Gray, 2020). AI also supports the progression towards more continuous, real-time auditing with increased forward-looking information (Moll & Yigitbasioglu, 2019).

It is clear that the accounting profession has embraced technology. With regard to data analytics and AI, some caution however is urged. It is acknowledged that while big data may act as a catalyst for transitioning accountants' roles, many accounting tasks are not easily automatable (Richins et al., 2017). Accumulating data is easy. Arguably, analysing data is also relatively easy. Effectively incorporating this data into an organisation's internal accounting procedures and practices requires proactive effort. This also necessitates education at a professional level in developing a stronger skill set in the techniques and technologies of big data in combination with the accountant's natural analytical skills (Chua & Lawson, 2015). In turn, AI undoubtedly enables accounting professionals to focus on higher level and more lucrative analysis, increasing efficiencies, improving judgement quality and reducing human error (Mosteanu & Faccia, 2020). However, the use of algorithms to make decisions does pose some questions about the extent to which accounting professionals versus the algorithms can be held accountable for ultimate outcomes in business or on audits (Court, 2015).

3.5 Re-imagining the Future of Work of Professionals

Professions play a key role in the implementation and operation of digital technologies in increasingly complex organisational settings. As they engage with these tools and techniques, they must be mindful that they are facilitating the programming of autonomous working tools and techniques to take over certain areas of activity and simultaneously creating new routines and work processes (Leitner-Hanetseder et al., 2021). However, digital technology brings with it serious challenges. But instead of framing these challenges as "inadequacies" or "failings", it may be more helpful to conceptualise digital technology as a disruption—a shift within the organisational field which each profession must acknowledge and respond to. Furthermore, new technology types are bringing about often subtle but far-reaching changes in the roles, identities and workflows of professionals within their given organisational field.

3.5.1 Technological Disruption

Let's revisit some of the key characteristics of professions outlined in Sect. 3.2 and consider their importance in the context of the disruptive technology discussed in Sect. 3.3. Professionals possess a body of proprietary knowledge or skill, and their power resides in their continued possession of that knowledge or skill as well as their control over who acquires it through admittance and continuing association with the profession. In addition, their status, authority and credibility are tied into a type of quality assurance which engenders a sense of trust and protects the public interest. What happens to this sense of trust in a profession increasingly enacted through AI? AI technology learns how to do its job better based on experience without the need to be repeatedly reprogrammed. It behaves independently of human oversight, responding to its environment and interacting with other technologies—learning, evolving and ultimately becoming further removed from its initial human design. It is questionable as to whether consumers of professional services will retain the same trust in a profession if the work is being carried out by technology that is becoming increasingly intelligent, autonomous and removed from human effort. If trust is to remain a cornerstone of what it means to be a professional, surely this will impose limits on the extent to which technologies such as AI can pervade professional services.

Staying with some of the key characteristics discussed in Sect. 3.2, professionals use judgement, flexibility and creativity in applying their specialist knowledge to specific and unique concerns and contexts. Yes, we have an exponential increase in data flows emerging from today's data-driven society, and certainly, technological solutions are critical in effectively capturing, mining and analysing the right data for every situation. But professionals offer advice and guidance having internalised their particular clients' determinants of a successful outcome. In this way, data is just one of several inputs into a decision-making process. Data analytics can certainly facilitate the nuanced and complex interrogation of data and machine learning can make predictions by categorising and sorting data and picking out patterns. But turning these analyses into professional advice and guidance requires the reflexive consideration of a combination of creative, intellectual and practical factors. This demands flexibility, reflexivity and judgement, which, so far, remain beyond the scope of technological solutions.

3.5.2 *The Professional's Evolving Organisational Field*

We cannot deny that professions are changing. The landscape within which professionals function is transforming, and while the issues discussed in the previous section might impose some parameters on the extent of change, technology is of course driving an ongoing redefining of the norms, values and beliefs to which professionals subscribe. This chapter allowed us to explore how organisational field members' (i.e., professionals) behaviours and roles are evolving in a gradual, almost unconscious way (Wooten & Hoffman, 2016).

We have seen throughout this chapter that changes within professions reflect broader changes in the business environment. Professions have traditionally traded on lofty attributes such as integrity, honesty and respect. However, the business models around these professionals have been forced to evolve, giving way to a more commercial focus dominated by an increasingly competitive professional services market which is as compelled as any industry to reduce its cost base and protect profit margins. This brings with it an obligation to ensure that regulation keeps pace with technological development (Kend & Nguyen, 2020). This changing professional services marketplace is evident, for example, in the growth in non-law businesses providing legal services and numerous 'off the shelf' accounting software packages. Technology is facilitating the automation and commoditisation of more routinised procedural tasks—disrupting current practices and at the same time creating new areas of competency. Those professionals who have taken a proactive approach and embraced new technologies at this level have thrived, and their increasing ability to deal with data and automate routine services has enabled them to widen their offerings, for example the shift of large accountancy firms to professional services firms (Shaffer et al., 2020). Within the legal sector, the shift is more gradual.

As discussed earlier in this chapter, novice professionals learn the fundamental aspects of their role carrying out basic routine tasks before ultimately progressing up the "tacit ladder" as they broaden their knowledge base and expand their skill set (Hager & Hodkinson, 2011, p. 64). If these routine tasks become increasingly automated, it begs the question "where do novice professionals learn the basics?" Perhaps they are playing a role in this automation process, creating in themselves a new area of technological competency which can be built on as their professional careers progress.

3.6 Challenges Ahead

Technology is becoming increasingly important and is driving the transformation and reconfiguration of knowledge, processes and offerings within professions. New specialist roles are emerging, including data curator and data analyst roles, to contend with the expanding data ecosystem, to harness content and to create pioneering solutions (Moll & Yigitbasioglu, 2019; WEF, 2018). Professionals face increasing pressure to develop competencies to bridge the gap between themselves and data analysts (Leitner-Hanetseder et al., 2021). This raises questions as to which further aspects of human work will and/or should be transferred to machines and which aspects will and/or should remain human-centric (Feeney, 2021; Walsh et al., 2019). It is important to remember that much of modern professional practice may not be facilitated by predetermined rules and decision trees but involves the ethics, identities and qualities of the individual professionals who deal with unique, uncertain, complex and ever-changing circumstances which necessitate a capacity to make creative professional judgements (Schon, 1983). Therefore, while human judgement will undoubtedly be further supplemented by technological advancement, it should not be replaced by an algorithm. Professions must be vigilant in developing the required skills, practices, competences and processes to remain relevant and add value (Moll & Yigitbasioglu, 2019). Individual professionals must continue to apply autonomy and reflexive consideration of practical, creative, and intellectual perspectives, as well as retain the capacity to form independent judgements which encompass changing particulars and contexts. They must remain accountable for the consequences, intended or otherwise, of their decisions (Court, 2015; Murphy & Rocchi, 2020). The key cornerstones of what it is to be a professional—that proprietary body of knowledge, trust, serving the public interest—have endured since the inception of professions hundreds of years ago and will continue to endure. Disruptive digital technologies simply represent the next stage in the lifecycle of professions. Professions must focus their renewed model around the changing environment, perhaps taking a leaf out of the tech companies' books. Tech companies are changing and adapting every day. Change in professional environments comes much more slowly, which is too slow for the world as it is now. What is currently a redefining of their role may be something more drastic in decades to come if relatively modest changes are not made now.

References

Alarie, B., Niblett, A., & Yoon, A. (2017). *How Artificial Intelligence will affect the practice of law (November)*. University of Toronto: Space Research Repository.

Alles, M. G., & Gray, G. L. (2020). Will the medium become the message? A framework for understanding the coming automation of the audit process. *Journal of Information Systems, 34*(2), 109–130.

Ayres, I., & Mitts, J. (2015). Anti-herding regulation. *Harvard Business Law Review, 5*(1), 18–20.

Baldwin, R. (2016). *The great convergence: Information technology and the new globalization*. Harvard University Press.

Bellman, R. (1978). *An introduction to Artificial Intelligence: Can computers think?* Boyd & Fraser Pub Co.

Bessen, J. (2018). *AI and jobs: The role of demand*. Working Paper National Bureau of Economic Research.

Blomgren, M., & Waks, C. (2015). Coping with contradictions: Hybrid professionals managing institutional complexity. *Journal of Professions & Organization, 2*(1), 78–102.

Boussard, V. (2018). Professional closure regimes in the global age: The boundary work of professional services specializing in mergers and acquisitions. *Journal of Professions and Organization, 5*(3), 279–296.

Brazel, J. F., & Agoglia, C. P. (2007). An examination of auditor planning judgements in a complex accounting information system environment. *Contemporary Accounting Research, 24*(4), 1059–1083.
Brock, D. M., Huseyin, L., & Muzio, D. (2014). Understanding professionals and their workplaces: The mission of the Journal of Professions and Organization. *Journal of Professions and Organization, 1*(1), 1–15.
Bromwich, M., & Bhimani, A. (1989). *Management accounting: Evolution not revolution*. Chartered Institute of Management Accountants (CIMA).
Bromwich, M., & Bhimani, A. (2009). *Management accounting: Retrospect and prospect*. Elsevier.
Brown, B., Chui, M., & Manyika, J. (2011). Are you ready for the era of 'Big Data?'. *The McKinsey Quarterly, Oct*, 24–35.
Bughin, J., Livingston, J., & Marwaha, S. (2011). Seizing the potential of 'Big Data'. *The McKinsey Quarterly, 4*, 103–109.
Burns, E. (2019). *Theorising professions: A sociological introduction*. Palgrave Macmillan.
Chiu, M., Manyika, J., & Miremadi, M. (2016). Where machines could replace humans- and where they can't (yet). *McKinsey Quarterly*, July.
Chua, F., & Lawson, R. (2015). *The data revolution*. The Association of Chartered Certified Accountants and Institute of Management Accountants. November.
Cooper, L. A., Holderness, D. K., Jr., Sorensen, T. L., & Wood, A. (2019). Robotic process automation in public accounting. *Accounting Horizons, 33*(4), 15–35.
Court, D. (2015). Getting big impact from big data. *The McKinsey Quarterly, 1*(1), 52–60.
Devins, C., Felin, T., Kauffman, S., & Koppl, R. (2017). The law and big data. *Cornell Journal of Law and Public Policy, 27*, 357–413.
Earley, C. (2015). Data analytics in auditing: Opportunities and challenges. *Business Horizons, 58*(5), 493–500.
Empson, L., Muzio, D., Broschak, J., & Hinings, B. (2015). Researching professional service firms: An introduction and overview. In L. Empson, D. Muzio, J. Broschak, & B. Hinings (Eds.), *Oxford handbook of professional service firms* (pp. 1–24). Oxford University Press.
Eraut, M. (1994). *Developing professional knowledge and competence*. RoutledgeFalmer.
Feeney, O. (2021). Accounting in a Social Context. In N. M. Alsharari (Ed.), *Accounting and Finance Innovations* (pp. 17–32). Intech Open.
Freidson, E. (1994). *Professionalism reborn: Theory, prophecy and policy*. Polity Press.
Frey, C. B., & Osborne, M. A. (2017). The future of employment: How susceptible are jobs to computerisation? *Technological Forecasting and Social Change, 114*, 254–280.

Hager, P., & Hodkinson, P. (2011). Becoming as an appropriate metaphor for understanding professional learning. In L. Scanlon (Ed.), *"Becoming a Professional": An interdisciplinary analysis of professional learning* (Lifelong learning book series) (Vol. 16, pp. 33–56). Springer.

Henke, N., Puri, A., & Saleh, T. (2020). Accelerating analytics to navigate COVID-19 and the next normal. *McKinsey.*

Institute of Chartered Accountants of England and Wales (ICAEW). (2014). *Big data and analytics—What's new?* ICAEW.

Karaca, K. (2021). Values and inductive risk in machine learning modelling: The case of binary classification models. *European Journal for Philosophy of Science, 11*(4), 1–27.

Kend, M., & Nguyen, L. A. (2020). Big data analytics and other emerging technologies: The impact on the Australian audit and assurance profession. *Australian Accounting Review, 30*(4), 269–282.

Leitner-Hanetseder, S., Lehner, O. M., Eisl, C., & Forstenlechner, C. (2021). A profession in transition: Actors, tasks and roles in AI-based accounting. *Journal of Applied Accounting Research, 22*(3), 539–555.

Liebowitz, J. (2020). *Data analytics and AI.* Auerbach Publications.

Loebbecke, C., & Picot, A. (2015). Reflections on societal and business model transformation arising from digitization and big data analytics: A research agenda. *The Journal of Strategic Information Systems, 24*(3), 149–157.

Merendino, A., Dibb, S., Meadows, M., Quinn, L., Wilson, D., Simkin, L., & Canhoto, A. (2018). Big data, big decisions: The impact of big data on board level decision-making. *Journal of Business Research, 93*, 67–78.

Moll, J., & Yigitbasioglu, O. (2019). The role of internet-related technologies in shaping the work of accountants: New directions for accounting research. *The British Accounting Review, 51*(6), 100833–100820.

Mosteanu, N. R., & Faccia, A. (2020). Digital systems and new challenges of financial management–FinTech, XBRL, blockchain and cryptocurrencies. *Quality-Access to Success Journal, 21*(174), 159–166.

Murphy, B., & Rocchi, M. (2020). Can accounting ethics be automated? *ACCA Accounting and Business Magazine*, October.

Nielsen, S. (2020). *Management accounting and the idea of machine learning.* Working Paper, Aarhus University.

Pakšiová, R., & Oriskóová, D. (2020). Capital maintenance evolution using outputs from accounting systems. *Scientific Annals of Economics and Business, 67*(3), 311–331.

Poole, D., Mackworth, A., & Goebel, R. (1998). *Computational intelligence: A logical approach.* Oxford University Press.

Rich, E., & Knight, K. S. (1991). *Artificial Intelligence* (2nd ed.). McGraw Hill.

Richins, G., Stapleton, A., Stratopoulos, T. C., & Wong, C. (2017). Big data analytics: Opportunity or threat for the accounting profession? *Journal of Information Systems, 31*(3), 63–79.

Russell, S., & Norvig, P. (2010). *Artificial Intelligence: A modern approach* (3rd ed.). University of California.

Schatzki, T. R. (2001). Introduction: Practice theory. In T. R. Schatzki, K. K. Cetina, & E. von Savigny (Eds.), *The practice turn in contemporary theory* (pp. 1–14). Routledge.

Schon, D. A. (1983). *The reflective practitioner: How professionals think in action.* Basic Books.

Shaffer, K. J., Gaumer, C. J., & Bradley, K. P. (2020). Artificial intelligence products reshape accounting: Time to re-train. *Development and Learning in Organizations: An International Journal, 34*(6), 41–43.

Susskind, D. (2021). *A world without work: Technology, automation and how we should respond.* Penguin Books.

Susskind, R. (2013). *Tomorrow's Lawyers: An introduction to your future.* Oxford University Press.

Susskind, R., & Susskind, D. (2015). *The future of professions: How technology will transform the work of human experts.* Oxford University Press.

Walsh, T., Levy, N., Bell, G., Elliott, A., Maclaurin, J., Mareels, I. M. Y., & Wood, F. M. (2019). *The effective and ethical development of artificial intelligence: An opportunity to improve our wellbeing.* Report for the Australian Council of Learned Academies.

Winston, P. H. (1992). *Artificial Intelligence.* Addison-Wesley Longman Publishing Co., Inc.

Wooten, M., & Hoffman, A. J. (2016). Organizational fields past, present and future. In R. Greenwood, C. Oliver, T. B. Lawrence, & R. R. Meyer (Eds.), *The Sage handbook of organizational institutionalism* (2nd ed., pp. 55–74). Sage.

World Economic Forum. (2018). *The future of jobs report.* World Economic Forum.

World Economic Forum. (2020). *The future of jobs report.* World Economic Forum.

Wu, L., Hitt, L., & Lou, B. (2020). Data analytics, innovation, and firm productivity. *Management Science, 66*, 1783–2290.

CHAPTER 4

Gig Work, Algorithmic Technologies, and the Uncertain Future of Work

James Duggan and Stefan Jooss

Abstract Throughout the last decade, the so-called gig economy has emerged as a disruptive and widely debated trend in the world of work. In this chapter, we trace the emergence of the gig economy from its inception during the global economic crisis to the present day where gig work arrangements span several sectors and face continuing scrutiny from critics. Specifically, we focus on the important role of algorithmic technologies in controlling the activities of gig workers and the subsequent challenges and controversies arising from the use of these new digital mechanisms. Finally, we identify the key implications arising from this new form of labour for workers, organisations, and regulatory bodies. In doing so, we explore a range of ongoing efforts to develop effective solutions for the various stakeholders involved.

J. Duggan (✉)
Cork University Business School, University College Cork, Cork, Ireland
e-mail: jamesduggan@ucc.ie

S. Jooss
UQ Business School, The University of Queensland, Brisbane, Australia
e-mail: s.jooss@uq.edu.au

T. Lynn et al. (eds.), *The Future of Work*, Palgrave Studies in Digital Business & Enabling Technologies,
https://doi.org/10.1007/978-3-031-31494-0_4

Keywords Gig economy • Gig work • Algorithmic technologies • Digital platforms • Managerial control

4.1 Introduction

Discussions of digital transformation in the workplace are far-reaching and explore a variety of perspectives, although much of this discourse tends to focus on the opportunities and challenges for more conventional forms of employment (Verhoef et al., 2021). Yet, throughout the last decade, a new body of research has emerged, which focuses exclusively on the implications of digitalisation and new technologies for atypical and contingent working arrangements—broadly recognised as causing the inception of the so-called gig economy (Adamson & Roper, 2010).

Conceptualisations of the gig economy have been relatively broad. Some define it as an umbrella term to encapsulate all forms of non-traditional, contingent, and less-structured work (Ashford et al., 2018). Others adopt a more focused perspective by viewing the gig economy as a new type of contingent work that is enabled and mediated via digital platform organisations, connecting on-demand workers with customers to perform fixed-term tasks (Barratt et al., 2020; Kuhn & Maleki, 2017). In this chapter, we subscribe to the latter perspective and consequently, conceptualise gig work as embracing some of the advanced capabilities of new technologies—such as machine learning and artificial intelligence (AI)—in creating service-providing digital infrastructures that thrive on connectivity (Duggan et al., 2020). Millions of gig workers around the world operate and earn a living from this novel form of work, often associated with well-known organisations such as Uber, Lyft, Deliveroo, Amazon Mechanical Turk, and Fiverr.

Given the breadth of services and sectors found in the gig economy, the proliferation of this labour form holds noteworthy consequences for the world of work. Although exact figures are difficult to source, by 2018 it was estimated that approximately 24 million people were engaged in some form of gig work across the European Union (Mariniello, 2021). The defining characteristic of gig work is that digital platform organisations match supply and demand between workers and users, rather than directly providing the services themselves (Tran & Sokas, 2017). Classified as independent contractors in almost all cases, gig workers are purportedly granted the freedom to work independently by controlling most aspects of the work, from scheduling to selecting tasks (Jabagi et al., 2019). Yet, perhaps the most controversial aspect of this work is the use of advanced algorithmic technologies to manage, monitor, and co-ordinate the activities of workers (Wood et al., 2019). This somewhat contradicts the supposed promise to "be your own boss" as self-employed freelancers. These technologies—collectively known as "algorithmic management"—are commonplace in most types of gig work (Walker et al., 2021).

In this chapter, we begin by tracing the emergence and continuing growth of the gig economy as a disruptive force in the labour market. Next, we examine the role of algorithmic technologies in enabling, shaping, and closely mediating gig working arrangements. Finally, we outline the most significant challenges and controversies associated with algorithmic management, while also exploring the potential to develop timely and effective solutions to these issues.

4.2 The Rise of the Gig Economy

Gig economy research indicates that atypical working arrangements first emerged around the time of the global economic crisis in 2008 (Tran & Sokas, 2017). The intense pressures faced by organisations during this period resulted in a shift away from the protections and security of conventional employment towards working arrangements that were more fragmented and precarious (Fleming, 2017). While some companies that are recognised as part of the gig economy started emerging slightly earlier (Amazon Mechanical Turk, for example, was launched in 2005), the "gig economy" moniker was coined by journalist Tina Brown in 2009 to describe variants of contingent work that are transacted exclusively via digital means, with each piece of work being akin to an individual "gig" (Tran & Sokas, 2017).

Throughout the last decade, the number and diversity of organisations operating in the gig economy has increased significantly (Poon, 2019), as has its popularity amongst users (Dupont et al., 2018). Often, the services available in the gig economy are resemblant of components of formerly full-time roles held by, for example, couriers, taxi drivers, or translators. Yet, in the gig economy, these roles have been fragmented into ad-hoc tasks, available on-demand and offered flexibly via digital technologies available on smart devices (Smith & Leberstein, 2015).

4.2.1 *The Unique Nature of Gig Work*

One of the main difficulties in studying gig work is that it encompasses a wide range of job types and working conditions (De Stefano, 2016). For example, many associate the gig economy with on-demand services in local markets, such as transportation with Uber or Lyft, or food delivery with Foodora or UberEats (McDonnell et al., 2021). Yet, gig work also includes remote, cloud-based crowdwork companies such as Fiverr and Amazon Mechanical Turk, who offer services such as transcription, translation, or survey design (Howcroft & Bergvall-Kåreborn, 2019). Some also refer to organisations such as Airbnb and Etsy, where individuals may sell goods or lease assets via platform organisations (Duggan et al., 2022a). However, the labour process involved in these organisations is less transparent, meaning it is more commonly associated with the "sharing economy", where digital platforms are used by individuals to sell goods or lease assets (Cheng & Foley, 2019).

Across all types of gig work, the intermediation of a digital platform to connect workers with customers or clients is shared (Newlands, 2021), as is the hyper-flexibility of the independent contractor status and the short-term nature of work assignments (Pichault & McKeown, 2019). Despite these shared characteristics, it is vital to recognise that there is substantial heterogeneity in the way gig work is designed, controlled, and organised across different job types and organisations (De Stefano, 2016). For example, some gig workers operate remotely and must actively search and bid for advertised projects (Howcroft & Bergvall-Kåreborn, 2019), while others are assigned specific on-demand tasks in local markets (Duggan et al., 2022b). Therefore, referring to gig work as a monolithic concept is problematic, most notably because this approach may create confusion about the appropriateness of the classification assigned to one type of gig work or the pervasiveness of algorithmic technologies used by certain digital platforms (McDonnell et al., 2021).

4.2.2 *The Role of Digital Platforms*

For platform organisations, the avoidance of the "employee" label in classifying gig workers is strategically important in removing the need for, among other things, potential overtime payments, union organisation, payroll taxes, and unemployment benefits. Platform organisations claim they "partner" with independent workers who offer their services to customers via digital platforms. A frequently cited example is Uber, which is regarded as the world's largest transportation company (although it is listed as Uber Technologies), yet the firm owns no vehicles (Duggan et al., 2022a). Similarly, Airbnb is larger than the world's top five hotel brands combined, with over 4 million listings worldwide, but owns no accommodation properties. While this concept may not seem entirely unusual in today's market, it nevertheless highlights the rapidly changing connectivity, technological disruption, and innovation that enabled the emergence of this business model.

However, a side-effect of this development is the creation of unique interdependencies and power dynamics between platform organisations and workers. Platform organisations have been accused of utilising questionable and controversial practices in managing gig workers, specifically in satisfying legal criteria to meet the independent contractor status, while simultaneously exerting significant control over workforces (Norlander et al., 2021). Research has consistently addressed and often supported this claim, suggesting that the reality of the working arrangement appears to be one where platform organisations avoid giving direct commands to workers, which may indicate a legal employment relationship, while simultaneously controlling the labour process by using algorithmic technologies (Wu et al., 2019). This context—where human managers are non-existent and potentially fierce competition exists between workers—is arguably not favourable to manifestations of workplace support or work-life balance, possibly yielding damaging outcomes for workers (Meijerink et al., 2021).

4.3 Algorithmic Technologies in Gig Work

A range of new technologies—such as analytics, machine learning, and AI—have become increasingly influential in transforming work and management practices (Schafheitle et al., 2020). Organisations have implemented technologies that can parse through large amounts of data, acquire skills and knowledge, and operate autonomously (Wang et al., 2020). In the context of gig work, we are especially concerned with how this innovation has allowed organisations to develop new, digitally enabled systems of control to comprehensively manage workforces. Ivanova et al. (2018) argue that understanding how strategies of managerial control have evolved with the advent of new technologies is key to understanding the future of workplace relations. The very nature of the algorithmic technologies utilised in gig work represents an intertwining of technology with the management function. In doing so, platform organisations create new, comprehensive forms of monitoring and micro-management that would be difficult to achieve in more conventional roles (Murray et al., 2021).

The algorithmic technologies used in gig work are designed to have agency over the labour process. This agency amounts to a temporally embedded capacity to intentionally constrain, complement, or substitute for humans in the practice of routines (Newlands, 2021). In doing so, these algorithms fundamentally alter our understanding of workplace management by determining protocols, rules, and guidelines for gig workers; by making decisions; and by encouraging specific actions (Kellogg et al., 2020). Research indicates that this is particularly common in local gig work, such as ridesharing and food delivery, but is also found in remote, cloud-based gig work (Duggan et al., 2020). Thus, the flexibility and independence that is seemingly afforded to gig workers is often heavily constrained through control systems that algorithmically structure and monitor workers' activities.

4.3.1 Algorithms and Managerial Control

Scholarship is increasingly concerned with understanding precisely how algorithms implement control over gig workers' activities (McDonnell et al., 2021; Schafheitle et al., 2020). The scenario is seemingly one where, at once, various algorithmic processes combine to limit the information that workers can access, place incentives on worker compliance, and pressurise workers to treat prompts as commands (Barratt et al., 2020). Controversially, algorithmic control systems are also characterised by their opaqueness, with research indicating that gig workers experience a lack of transparency over how they are being monitored, ranked, and assessed (Cheng & Foley, 2019; Duggan et al., 2022b).

Thus, despite enabling the efficient organisation and delivery of work, there are concerns about the implications of algorithmic control for individual workers (Kellogg et al., 2020). This is because algorithmic management is primarily focused on the provision of instrumental support, leaving little room for worker engagement or the formation of meaningful social relationships (Ivanova et al., 2018). Accordingly, many of our traditional assumptions about the social aspects of work are considered obsolete, or perhaps even counterproductive, as these would potentially disrupt the monitoring and matching capabilities of the algorithm (Murray et al., 2021).

4.3.2 *Algorithmic Management in Practice*

Gig economy researchers have drawn on various theories in efforts to effectively understand the role of algorithmic technologies in organising labour (Gandini, 2019; Veen et al., 2020). It is argued that the platform organisation and its architecture, in the form of algorithmic technologies and digital platforms (i.e., smartphone applications or websites), should be understood as a digital-based point of production (Gandini, 2019)—in other words, the novel, unique 'place' where the labour process is enacted and where social relations are repurposed. Such perspectives, with the experiences of gig workers at the centre of the analysis, are seen as being valuable in advancing knowledge in this domain.

In seeking to understand the role of algorithms in implementing control, Kellogg et al. (2020) identify the various directional, evaluation, and disciplinary strategies enabled by these technologies. The outcome is that algorithmic control reconfigures working relations in several ways. This includes prompting workers to make specific decisions preferred by the organisation; restricting the availability of information to prevent specific behaviours; evaluating workers' activities by recording and aggregating performance metrics and data; rating and ranking workers' performance to guide future behaviour; and disciplining workers by potentially deactivating underperforming workers, while rewarding others with enhanced flexibility and bonus payments (Kellogg et al., 2020). Based on this, algorithmic management appears to be comprehensive, instantaneous, and hyper-efficient when compared to traditional means of control (McDonnell et al., 2021). Yet, long-term effectiveness of this has been called into question, particularly within the strategic context of engaging with and motivating workers (Jabagi et al., 2019).

4.4 Algorithms and Gig Work: Challenges, Controversies, and Uncertainties

The risks of gig work have been well documented, both in scholarly literature and policy reports (Duggan et al., 2022b; Taylor et al., 2017). The scope of these risks is quite extensive and spans an array of disciplinary perspectives. Yet, the core issue underpinning most of the ongoing research in this sphere—regardless of the discipline—is whether gig work is good or bad. Specifically, is gig work exploitative? Is the independent contractor classification unfair? Are algorithmic technologies being used inappropriately? If the answer to any of these questions is "yes", how can we solve these issues and create a gig economy that works for all stakeholders?

4.4.1 *Challenges for Management Practice*

For digital platform organisations, the use of algorithmic management undoubtedly increases efficiency, reduces risks, and decreases labour costs—at least in the short term (Walker et al., 2021). Likewise, for gig workers, limited research indicates that algorithmic management grants a degree of autonomy and independence in scheduling and completing work (Duggan et al., 2022b; Meijerink & Bondarouk, 2021). Yet, research predominantly indicates that these technologies create complex challenges for workers via their capacity to dramatically alter the power dynamics between workers and organisations (Schafheitle et al., 2020). The data-dominated approach to managerial responsibility potentially moves gig work into an inhuman form, with algorithms undertaking roles that were traditionally the preserve of supervisors or managers, and with workers being disciplined or penalised in real-time (Norlander et al., 2021).

Management scholars continue to debate the long-term implications of algorithmic technologies, particularly if those practices currently normalised in gig work were to spread to more conventional forms of employment. There are arguments that the monitoring and surveillance capabilities of algorithmic management are contributing to the creation of a contemporary form of scientific management (McGaughey, 2018): jobs are fragmented into simple and repetitive tasks; the labour process is tightly controlled to ensure maximum efficiency; and workers who underperform can be easily identified and replaced (Duggan et al., 2022a). Thus, organisations can guarantee a high degree of consistency and predictability in the services delivered. However, while highly standardised processes may limit the risk of error, such rigidity also tends to increase work arduousness and inhibit professional growth (Jürgens et al., 1993). The "duality" of algorithmic management (Meijerink & Bondarouk, 2021)—both restraining and enabling value for workers—clearly brings the need for a more critical consideration of the implications and consequences for employment relations and the management function.

4.4.2 *Challenges for Legislators and Policymakers*

The gig economy has altered business models and confounded established people management structures, thereby requiring new ways of thinking about the dynamics that may potentially reshape workplaces. The classification of gig workers as independent contractors is undoubtedly a significant, ongoing challenge for regulatory bodies. To date, proposed solutions are less than straightforward. For example, a commonly cited suggestion is to reclassify all gig workers as employees, thereby providing the protections and benefits that accompany employment. However, this would eradicate the flexibility enjoyed by many gig workers, while also upending the operating model of most gig organisations (Cappelli & Keller, 2013). Others have proposed the creation of a special employment status for gig workers, in recognition that these arrangements do not fully align with either the definition of employees or the self-employed (Taylor et al., 2017). The complexity of this issue is illustrated by the varying rulings of courts on the same issue over the last number of years, perhaps indicating that a universal solution does not exist (Duggan et al., 2022a).

Within the European Union, consultations are currently taking place regarding the development of new instruments to effectively regulate gig work (Hauben et al., 2020). However, regulating digital platform organisations has proven to be a complex task, and policymakers will require an in-depth understanding of how the gig economy is shaping the labour market and working conditions to develop effective measures tailored to different forms of gig work (Duggan et al., 2022a). This calls for a close collaboration between researchers and policymakers, who should combine forces to further our understanding of the advantages and challenges posed by the gig economy.

4.4.3 *Uncertainties for Workers*

By not belonging to a particular organisation or a continuous, bounded occupational group, gig workers find themselves in what Ibarra and Obodaru (2016) call a 'liminal space' between occupations: immersed in hyper-flexibility, completing short-term assignments, and only offered work on a task-by-task basis. The very nature of gig work is that most tasks are performed individually, in isolation, without contact with fellow workers and often in competition with them (McGaughey, 2018). This leads to weak social ties and forms perhaps the largest obstacle for individuals seeking to craft a more meaningful working arrangement (Wang et al., 2020).

Gig work also presents challenges for workers' abilities to develop career-related skills and competencies. Ostensibly, the autonomy and flexibility promised by gig work seems appealing, where workers can freely move across organisations in developing their professional skills. However, Bérastégui (2021) argues that the apparent fluidity of the gig economy is at best illusory, and at worst like "quicksand", trapping individuals in a cycle of financial vulnerability and low-skilled work without professional stability. Research indicates that although some may have alternative career options or may enjoy their working arrangement, a longer-term implication is the difficulty for workers to effectively disengage from the gig economy due to a lack of financial security and the inability to develop professional skills (Duggan et al., 2022b).

With some evidence that gig work has started to emerge in wider professional areas such as finance, graphic design, and software coding (Minifie, 2016), these issues highlight the importance of creating a gig economy where decent work can flourish and where arrangements represent a stepping-stone for workers to progress their careers. Yet, caution must be exercised by not assuming that the experiences of all gig workers are homogenous. Instead, organisations and policymakers must work towards achieving a fuller understanding of the individual motivations and experiences of gig workers. If more workers are poised to join the gig economy in some capacity, the current operating model poses significant issues for workers via the lack of opportunities to reskill or upskill through their work.

4.5 Conclusion

As more research becomes available, it seems increasingly likely that the perceived independence from managerial control in gig work does not necessarily result in increased autonomy for workers—at least not to the extent promised by platform organisations (Maffie, 2020). This instigates the need for further studies to determine to what extent different types of gig workers lack various forms of support (e.g., career mentoring, coaching, and collegial or task support) and which aspects of gig work are most detrimental to this. The Covid-19 pandemic has cast new light on the essential nature of many gig workers, while also demonstrating that these workers, in many ways, are the guinea pigs of the new world of work.

Likewise, the pandemic also escalated concerns that some aspects of this hyper-flexible, precarious labour form may go mainstream sooner than expected, reinforcing the need for more research and refined policy considerations.

References

Adamson, M., & Roper, I. (2010). Good jobs and bad jobs: Contemplating job quality in different contexts. *Work, Employment and Society, 33*(4), 551–559.

Ashford, S., Caza, B., & Reid, E. (2018). From surviving to thriving in the gig economy: A research agenda for individuals in the new world of work. *Research in Organizational Behaviour, 38*, 23–41.

Barratt, T., Goods, C., & Veen, A. (2020). 'I'm my own boss...': Active intermediation and 'entrepreneurial' worker agency in the Australian gig economy. *EPA: Economy and Space, 52*(8), 1643–1661.

Bérastégui, P. (2021). *Exposure to psychological risk factors in the gig economy: A systematic review*. European Trade Union Institute.

Cappelli, P., & Keller, J. R. (2013). Classifying work in the new economy. *Academy of Management Review, 38*(4), 575–596.

Cheng, M., & Foley, C. (2019). Algorithmic management: The case of Airbnb. *International Journal of Hospitality Management, 83*, 33–36.

De Stefano, V. (2016). *The rise of the 'just-in-time' workforce: On-demand work, crowdwork and labour protection in the gig economy*. International Labour Office.

Duggan, J., Sherman, U., Carbery, R., & McDonnell, A. (2020). Algorithmic management and app-work in the gig economy: A research agenda for employment relations and HRM. *Human Resource Management Journal, 30*(1), 114–132.

Duggan, J., McDonnell, A., Sherman, U., & Carbery, R. (2022a). *Work in the gig economy: A research overview*. Routledge.

Duggan, J., Sherman, U., Carbery, R., & McDonnell, A. (2022b). Boundaryless careers and algorithmic constraints in the gig economy. *The International Journal of Human Resource Management, 33*(22), 4468–4498.

Dupont, J., Hughes, S., Wolf, R., & Wride, S. (2018). *Freedom and flexibility: The relationship deliveroo riders have with the labour market*. Public First.

Fleming, P. (2017). The human capital hoax: Work, debt and insecurity in the era of Uberization. *Organisation Studies, 38*(5), 691–709.

Gandini, A. (2019). Labour process theory and the gig economy. *Human Relations, 72*(6), 1039–1056.

Hauben, H., Lenaerts, K., & Wayaert, W. (2020). *The platform economy and precarious work*. European Parliament Committee on Employment and Social Affairs.

Howcroft, D., & Bergvall-Kåreborn, B. (2019). A typology of crowdwork platforms. *Work, Employment and Society, 33*(1), 21–38.

Ibarra, H., & Obodaru, O. (2016). Betwixt and between identities: Liminal experience in contemporary careers. *Research in Organizational Behaviour, 36*(1), 47–64.

Ivanova, M., Bronowicka, J., Kocher, J., & Degner, A. (2018). *The app as a boss? Control and autonomy in application-based management*. European University Viadrina.

Jabagi, N., Croteau, A., Audebrand, L., & Marsan, J. (2019). Gig workers' motivation: Thinking beyond carrots and sticks. *Journal of Managerial Psychology, 34*(4), 192–213.

Jürgens, U., Malsch, T., & Dohse, K. (1993). *Breaking from Taylorism: Changing forms of work in the automobile industry*. Cambridge University Press.

Kellogg, K., Valentine, M., & Christin, A. (2020). Algorithms at work: The new contested terrain of control. *Academy of Management Annals, 14*(1), 366–410.

Kuhn, K., & Maleki, A. (2017). Micro-entrepreneurs, dependent contractors, and instaserfs: Understanding online labour platform workforces. *Academy of Management Perspectives, 31*(3), 183–200.

Maffie, M. (2020). The role of digital communities in organising gig workers. *Industrial Relations: A Journal of Economy and Society, 59*(1), 123–149.

Mariniello, M. (2021). An inclusive European Union must boost gig workers' rights. *Bruegel*, 7 December.

McDonnell, A., Carbery, R., Burgess, J., & Sherman, U. (2021). Technologically mediated human resource management in the gig economy. *The International Journal of Human Resource Management, 32*(19), 3995–4015.

McGaughey, E. (2018). Taylorooism: When network technology meets corporate power. *Industrial Relations Journal, 49*(5–6), 459–472.

Meijerink, J., & Bondarouk, T. (2021). The duality of algorithmic management: Toward a research agenda on HRM algorithms, autonomy and value creation. *Human Resource Management Review*.

Meijerink, J., Keegan, A., & Bondarouk, T. (2021). Having their cake and eating it too? Online labor platforms and human resource management as a case of institutional complexity. *The International Journal of Human Resource Management, 32*(19), 4016–4052.

Minifie, J. (2016). *Peer to peer pressure: Policy for the sharing economy*. Eurofound.

Murray, A., Rhymer, J., & Sirmon, D. (2021). Humans and technology: Forms of conjoined agency in organizations. *Academy of Management Review, 46*(3), 130–149.

Newlands, G. (2021). Algorithmic surveillance in the gig economy: The organisation of work through Lefebvrian conceived space. *Organisation Studies, 42*(5), 719–737.

Norlander, P., Jukic, N., Varma, A., & Nestorov, S. (2021). The effects of technological supervision on gig workers: Organizational control and motivation of

Uber, taxi, and limousine drivers. *The International Journal of Human Resource Management, 32*(19), 4053–4077.

Pichault, F., & McKeown, T. (2019). Autonomy at work in the gig economy: Analysing work status, work content and working conditions of independent professionals. *New Technology, Work and Employment, 34*(1), 59–72.

Poon, T. (2019). Independent workers: Growth trends, categories, and employee relations implications in the emerging gig economy. *Employee Responsibilities and Rights Journal, 31*(1), 63–69.

Schafheitle, S., Weibel, A., Ebert, I., Kaspet, G., Schank, C., & Leicht-Deobald, U. (2020). No stone left unturned? Towards a framework for the impact of datafication technologies on organizational control. *Academy of Management Discoveries, 6*(3), 455–487.

Smith, R., & Leberstein, S. (2015). *Rights on demand: Ensuring workplace standards and worker security in the on-demand economy.* National Employment Law Project.

Taylor, M., Marsh, G., Nicol, D., & Broadbent, P. (2017). *Good work: The Taylor review of modern working practices.* Department of Business, Energy, and Industry.

Tran, M., & Sokas, R. (2017). The gig economy and contingent work: An occupational health assessment. *Journal of Occupational and Environmental Medicine, 59*(4), 63–66.

Veen, A., Barratt, T., & Goods, C. (2020). Platform-capital's appetite for control: A labour process analysis of food-delivery work in Australia. *Work, Employment and Society, 34*(3), 388–406.

Verhoef, P. C., Broekhuizen, T., Bart, Y., Bhattacharya, A., Dong, J. Q., Fabian, N., & Haenlein, M. (2021). Digital transformation: A multidisciplinary reflection and research agenda. *Journal of Business Research, 122*, 889–901.

Walker, M., Fleming, P., & Berti, M. (2021). 'You can't pick up a phone and talk to someone': How algorithms function as biopower in the gig economy. *Organisation, 28*(1), 26–43.

Wang, B., Liu, Y., & Parker, S. (2020). How does the use of information communication technology affect individuals: A work design perspective. *Academy of Management Annals, 14*(2), 695–725.

Wood, A., Graham, M., Lehdonvirta, V., & Hjorth, I. (2019). Good gig, bad gig: Autonomy and algorithmic control in the global gig economy. *Work, Employment and Society, 33*(1), 56–75.

Wu, O., Zhang, H., Li, Z., & Liu, K. (2019). Labor control in the gig economy: Evidence from Uber in China. *Journal of Industrial Relations, 61*(4), 574–596.

CHAPTER 5

Smart Technology in the Workplace: Threats and Opportunities for Trusting Employers

Xuchang Zheng, Simon Daniel Schafheitle, and Lisa van der Werff

Abstract In this chapter, we discuss the implications of how smart technology is experienced in the workplace for employee trust. Focusing on the defining features of smart technology and how these influence social interaction, we explore how trends in the permeation of technology in workplaces can influence employee trust in their employers creating both threats and opportunities for trust in this relationship. Realising the benefits of technological development requires employees to trust the intentions and capability of their employers to manage smart technology in ways that protect employee interests. We highlight the features of smart technology that may hamper this trust and discuss how addressing

X. Zheng (✉) • L. van der Werff
DCU Business School, Dublin City University, Dublin, Ireland
e-mail: xuchang.zheng@dcu.ie; lisa.vanderwerff@dcu.ie

S. D. Schafheitle
University of St. Gallen, St. Gallen, Switzerland
e-mail: simondaniel.schafheitle@unisg.ch

T. Lynn et al. (eds.), *The Future of Work*, Palgrave Studies in Digital Business & Enabling Technologies,
https://doi.org/10.1007/978-3-031-31494-0_5

concerns related to data privacy, situational normality, structural assurance, and employees' participation in the process is crucial for protecting and building trust in the workplace.

Keywords Smart technology • Trust • Organisation • Data privacy • Situational normality • Structural assurance • Employee participation

5.1 Introduction

The rapid growth of enterprise digital technology adoption has an increasing influence on organisational life impacting all stages of the employee life cycle (Schneider & Sting, 2020; von Krogh, 2018). In this chapter, we discuss how the use of digital technology in workplaces is critical to employee trust in their employing organisation. Useful reviews of the functioning logics and technological specificities of machine learning (ML) and deep learning (DL) algorithms can be found elsewhere (Alloghani et al., 2020; Jordan & Mitchell, 2015). In contrast, our focus in this chapter is on employees' experiences of technology and how cutting-edge technologies such as algorithm-based applications might become perceptible and tangible in organisations on a day-to-day-basis. Specifically, we highlight the trust impact of such technology through the lens of its socio-technological materialisations.

The remainder of this chapter considers employee trust in organisations in the context of smart technology. We outline why trust is critical to the success of smart technology adoption in the workplace before discussing challenges for protecting trust in employers in a technology-rich environment and opportunities for building employee trust in their organisation.

5.2 Employees' Trust in Organisations and Smart Technology

Trust, as a willingness to be vulnerable based on positive expectations of others, is often described as the foundation of social interaction (Lewis & Weigert, 2012; Mayer et al., 1995) or the lubricant that allows people to effectively interact and collaborate (Simpson, 2007). In the context of an organisation, trust is vital in facilitating effective interaction between co-workers, teams, and departments, as well as across these levels (Gillespie et al., 2021).

Employees' trust in their employer refers to the whole entity of the employing organisation as the target of trust (Fulmer & Gelfand, 2012). Similar to trust in individuals (McKnight et al., 1998), the foundation of employees' trust in their employer can be broadly categorised into two domains (Mishina et al., 2012). The first aspect relates to the character of the organisation: what the organisation *intends* to do. It is usually reflected as an organisation's goals, preferences, and values (e.g., Love & Kraatz, 2009) and has close parallels with benevolence and integrity (Mayer et al., 1995). In the context of technology implementation, for instance, trust in the character of the organisation may influence whether employees infer that the goal of introducing new technology is to yield labour cost-savings or to provide additional staff support. The second aspect concerns employees' assessments of employer capability or competence: what the organisation *can* do (Mishina et al., 2012). Depending on the nature of the task in question, the capability of the employer may be assessed based on the knowledge or resources that enable the organisation to fulfil its goal. The question of whether introducing novel technologies in the workplace facilitates or complicates the distribution of resources or the outcome of employees' work remains particularly relevant given the broadened options available to the employer. Particularly in times of rapid change, uncertainty regarding an employer's character or capability can create doubts and anxieties that hamper trust in the employer and create resistance to the adoption of these unfamiliar methods and patterns of work.

Scholarly and industry sources repeatedly identify effective technology deployment in workplaces as being a critical challenge for firms over the next decade (Van den Heuvel & Bondarouk, 2017). Trust is vital in facilitating effective workplace interactions (Fulmer & Gelfand, 2012), allowing organisations to function successfully (Weibel et al., 2016), and to deploy technology smoothly (Bain & Taylor, 2000). Employee trust is crucial to the successful deployment of smart technologies, especially those involving ML/DL, as it shapes both the way employees are managed and their reaction to change (Zirkle & Staples, 2005; Bain & Taylor, 2000). Given the increasing uncertainty associated with the changing efficiency and patterns of the work that new technology can bring, a more nuanced understanding of technology's trust impact is critical (Lynn et al., 2021; van der Werff et al., 2021). In this chapter, we frame technology deployment effectiveness as a social process facilitated by a mutual awareness and protection of trust between the employee and employer.

Smart technology becomes a tangible part of employees' workplace experiences via two socio-technological materialisations: (1) appropriateness and (2) foresightedness (Nilsson, 2014). Using the example of a pocket calculator to illustrate the appropriateness of smart technology (Stone et al., 2018), smart technology functions appropriately because, compared to humans, it performs complex calculations faster, more precisely, and with a much lower probability of error. However, facilitating the accuracy and efficiency of work by itself is not sufficient to be called a smart technology. The other crucial condition for technology to be perceived as smart is foresightedness, which helps refine work without human intervention (Chakraborty et al., 2017). Foresight, based on the various forms of supervised and unsupervised ML/DL, enables technology to autonomously "get better at what it does" and thus to apply its technological capabilities to the original but also to related and novel questions. IBM's Watson algorithm is an intuitive example of this. Although it was initially trained to recognise dog motifs from a large number of pictures, it is now employed to perform a wide range of other tasks including filtering future high potentials from a large number of job applications. It is this foresightedness of smart technology that brings out the potential for automation, not only with regard to work execution but also to aspects of leadership. Often this foresightedness creates anxiety and heightened vulnerability for humans interacting with the technology due to a lack of understanding and transparency regarding how particular decisions are made (Orlikowski & Scott, 2014; Nilsson, 2014).

Smart technology draws on developments in ML/DL processes and can be used within the employment relationship to (1) assist and support organisations in directing employees' attention, motivating or encouraging them to act in desirable ways, and (2) enable new ways of doing so, that have not been possible in the analogue world (Cardinal et al., 2010; Schafheitle et al., 2020). For instance, Gloor et al. (2018) have demonstrated how virtual mirroring (i.e., technology that captures communication behaviour including "between the lines") helps employees to adapt their communication styles to their peers' needs and supports leaders in designing employee needs-based development plans. Other examples of smart technology application in the employment relationship range from algorithmic automation of shortlisting as a part of the recruiting process (Hunkenschroer & Luetge, 2022), performance monitoring and evaluation software (Ravid et al., 2020), "smart" feedback solutions with algorithmic nudging capabilities for leaders (Buck & Morrow, 2018) to virtual career assistants which help employees increase their promotability, job mobility, and personal development (Stieglitz et al., 2021).

The potential benefits of smart technology application in these situations are increasingly clear; however, given the importance of trust in technology adoption and organisational change more generally, realising those benefits requires organisations and their leaders to be cognisant of how smart technology can influence trust in the organisation. The extent to which smart workplace technology changes the levels of risk and trust employees experience in their organisation depends on the design and functionality of the technology in question. Common practices of advocating the technological strengths of smart technology, in particular relative to human performance in the workplace, is unlikely to be effective as it does little to support perceptions of organisational character or capability. In the remainder of this chapter, we explore the challenges and opportunities that smart technology poses for trust between employees and their organisations.

5.3 Challenges for Protecting Trust in the Organisation

Two of the key reasons why employees' trust in their employing organisation might be strained by smart technology deployment broadly relate to how employee perceptions of their organisation's character are influenced by changes in visibility and accountability and interest alignment. Specifically, employees' perceptions of the employer's character, which are challenged by technology-heightened levels of employee visibility that highlight power differentials and vulnerabilities in the relationship, relate to benevolence. Similar character perceptions regarding employer integrity may become strained given changes in interactions between employees and their leaders that highlight differences in accountability and interest alignment within the workplace.

Smart technology use in the employment relationship creates enormous quantities of data about employee behaviour. This process frames employees as data subjects which may hamper employee trust because it makes them more visible inside the organisation (Stanton & Stam, 2006). More precisely, it increases the overall workplace transparency by transforming the formerly unmeasurable into measurable quantities. In the words of Bernstein (2017, p. 218), increased workplace transparency can be summarised in the following four exemplary statements: "Let us all see your activity" (i.e., technology-augmented monitoring), "Watch our workflow" (i.e., technology-augmented process visibility), "We're watching everything you do" (i.e., technology-enabled workplace surveillance), and "Let me tell you about your work" (i.e., technology-enabled disclosure of novel or hitherto unmeasurable employee information).

Smart technology allows organisations to gather and interpret employee performance data not only through log-in times, mouse pointer movements, or URL-/logfile evaluations but also through more invasive methods including recording eye movements in human-machine interaction, wearable robotics (e.g., fatigue measurement through exoskeletons), or Internet-of-Things applications, including wearable GPS devices or bio-radio frequency identity (RFID) chips. For instance, "smart chairs" and CO_2 measurements enable the collection of performance data, such as when employees are most productive (e.g., Wang & MacLellan, 2018), or "smart toilets" enable the collection of health data as a means to later evaluate promotion opportunities (e.g., Petre, 2018). Recently, Hong Kong engineers have started to analyse executive-level board members' brain activity during C-suite meetings to decipher the success formula of effective corporate governance (Copeland & Hope, 2016).

Compared to the more traditional working environment, the technology-augmented information acquisition and analysis of employee data can challenge trust in two ways. Firstly, technology can challenge employee beliefs about what they can expect from the employment relationship and how central they are in the organisation's priorities. The implementation of new technology can be framed either as intending to enable employees or as an attempt to create a foolproof organisation in a way that alienates employees and leads to feelings of coercion (Adler & Borys, 1996). Second, the change to processes that accompanies technology deployment in the workplace can negatively affect employee perceptions of situational normality and that everything is "as it should be". Technology proliferation that increases visibility, for instance, influences employees' feelings of vulnerability due to being monitored by the employer in a way that is likely to make them more alert and careful in their workplace interactions. Finally, as with many change initiatives, introducing new smart technology in the workplace can trigger suspicion in management's intention in implementing these changes. Specifically, employer collection of data sources such as feelings, relationship qualities, and other previously relatively personal information either conveys that the employer suspects bad or dishonest intentions of employees or intends to use this information as a trust substitute (Falk & Kosfeld, 2006; Lockey et al., 2021; Whitener et al., 1998). Secondly, technology functions related to decision selection and action implementation raise issues related to accountability and interest alignment that are likely to affect perceptions of the capability of the manager and the employer. Even when the digitised decision and action process is designed to support the manager's own job (Murray et al., 2021), employees may still question the manager's control of the technology and how they will be affected by the change. Will my manager be persuaded by the recommendations or decisions of technology that might negatively affect my performance appraisal? The use of information in this way implies a change to established ways of interacting between employees and employers.

Schafheitle et al. (2021) have argued that smart technology deployment leads to the increasing automation of leadership, even for those tasks that were previously believed to remain in the "human turf". For instance, media reports of such technologies note its ability to secretly nudge other people, to emotionally trigger them (Meckel, 2018), or to tell funny jokes (Gloor et al., 2018). Schafheitle et al. (2021) outline three trust-critical scenarios: a continuous blurring of responsibilities, conflicting directives of human managers and algorithms, and the fraternisation or co-option of the human manager and the algorithm against the employee. This first scenario is trust-critical because it increases uncertainty for employees. Questions similar to "To whom am I responsible?", "Why do I always have to take the rap?", "Does my manager still envisage the 'right' goals?", or "Can I be sure that they will always act in ways to protect my interests?", are likely to emerge. The second scenario becomes tangible if one considers that the most accurate decision is not always the "best" one for the company. For instance, it might be appropriately calculated that an employee fails to meet a certain email frequency threshold for qualifying as an internal expert, but they might be offering advice and/or mentoring support face-to-face, always having an open ear or offering support via their physical and emotional presence. The third scenario is well-entitled as "human oversight" where managers "blindly rely" on algorithmic feedback and, more or less explicitly, negate to include contextual information for managerial sense-making.

Focusing on the needs of the organisation but overlooking the concerns of the employee, smart technology designed either for decision support or implementation via various individual channels can be perceived by employees to be particularly threatening. Further, for employees, if smart technology interferes with human decision-making and implementation, it is likely to be perceived as contrasting the existing pattern of work, which tends to lower trust in the manager and the employee's subsequent willingness to accept the change proposed. For organisations, balancing between the needs for more detailed information about employees and the complex functioning of smart technology and anticipated employee resistance is key to the success of maintaining trust and introducing these changes in the workplace. Therefore, the question remains: how can effective smart technology implementation be achieved without threatening employment relationships?

5.4 Opportunities for Building Trust in the Organisation

Examining this issue from a trust perspective, we look to opportunities for organisations to implement smart technology in ways that are more protective and supportive of trust. In particular, theory suggests that careful attention to issues of data privacy, situational normality, structural assurance, and employee participation are likely to be vital. We provide some exploration of these protective measures below though further research is necessary to determine the efficacy and boundary conditions of these measures for protecting employee trust during the proliferation of smart technology in our workplaces.

Protecting data privacy by minimising the visibility of an individual footprint in the process of smart technology deployment is crucial for retaining employee trust while implementing the change (Stanton & Stam, 2006). The anonymisation of employee data starting from the earlier stages (e.g., data collection) and covering more stages of the overall technology deployment process can help to address employees' concerns. If anonymity cannot be guaranteed, organisations are particularly prone to the loss of trust.

Further, as members of the same organisation, employees' interpretation of managers' and colleagues' trustworthiness can be enhanced by giving a sense of situational normality (McKnight et al., 1998). If the way work is carried out appears to be "normal" and "in proper order" even after smart technology deployment (Baer et al., 2018; Lewis & Weigert, 1985), employees may reasonably rely on their past positive experience to infer that managers will continue to behave in a similarly normal and predictable manner. For organisations, with the adoption of smart technology becoming the new norm, the restoration of a sense of normality is crucial for trust to grow and flourish within the organisation. Employees who are comfortable with their own role and the purpose of smart technology, knowing the latter's introduction will support rather than replace their job, are more likely to maintain trust in the employer.

Providing structural assurance, such as regulatory or social safeguards, that reinforces any claims made by management is a useful channel for enhancing trust, especially at the initial introduction of the new technology rather than later (McKnight et al., 1998). Structural assurance that focuses on stipulating the actions of management, for instance, professional membership or organisational policies that prescribe adherence to a clear set of ethical norms, is powerful for encouraging acceptance of new technology (Long & Sitkin, 2018). Employees feel more assured about the intentions of managers when the potential cost of any untrustworthy behaviour such as misconduct or exploitation is higher than its reward. On the other hand, positive structural reinforcement, such as rewards for successful utilisation of new technology in the workplace, provides another incentive for employees to experience and verify the authenticity of their manager's words.

Lastly, highlighting the employer's control over decision selection and action implementation processes is crucial for maintaining an overall sense of normality within the organisation. Even when smart technology automates decision and action implementation, managers may emphasise and clarify "human logic" as the foundation of automation. For instance, a group understanding or consensus in relation to automation must be achieved for it to be enacted (Murray et al., 2021). Alternatively, any decision or action taken via automation may be approved and announced by managers instead of being implemented without scrutiny. To be perceived as a supporting function rather than the actual agent of decisions is crucial for the acceptance of automation by employees, before the change becomes the new norm within the organisation. Similar to Feldman's assertions that organisational theory holds "so long as human agents perform them" (2000, p. 627), an employee's trust holds when they perceive human, not smart technology, to be the true leader who ultimately determines the process and outcome in the workplace (Schafheitle et al., 2021).

The potential for smart technology to make work easier and more efficient through greater transparency, efficient knowledge management, and learning has been repeatedly demonstrated. Yet, its initial success in sociotechnological materialisations hinges on whether the technology builds an employee's confidence in the character and capability of the organisation rather than, or at least as well as, the technology itself. For management, clarifying intentions and providing assurance in relation to the purpose of the new technology may be even more crucial for protecting and building trust than advocating its technological strengths and benefits. Besides the various pay-offs associated with successful tango of smart technology and trust in the workplace, companies might also consider trust protection as a normative principle, since trust, personal growth, and flourishing have been established as virtues of modern work.

References

Adler, P. S., & Borys, B. (1996). Two types of bureaucracy: Enabling and coercive. *Administrative Science Quarterly, 41*(1), 61–89.

Alloghani, M., Al-Jumeily, D., Mustafina, J., Hussain, A., & Aljaaf, A. J. (2020). A systematic review on supervised and unsupervised machine learning algorithms for data science. In *Supervised and unsupervised learning for data science*, 3–21. Springer.

Baer, M. D., Van Der Werff, L., Colquitt, J. A., Rodell, J. B., Zipay, K. P., & Buckley, F. (2018). Trusting the "look and feel": Situational normality, situational aesthetics, and the perceived trustworthiness of organizations. *Academy of Management Journal, 61*(5), 1718–1740.

Bain, P., & Taylor, P. (2000). Entrapped by the 'electronic panopticon'? Worker resistance in the call centre. *New Technology, Work and Employment, 15*(1), 2–18.

Bernstein, E. S. (2017). Making transparency transparent: The evolution of observation in management theory. *Academy of Management Annals, 11*(1), 217–266.

Buck, B., & Morrow, J. (2018). AI, performance management and engagement: Keeping your best their best. *Strategic HR Review, 17*(5), 261–262.

Cardinal, L. B., Sitkin, S. B., & Long, C. P. (2010). A configurational theory of control. In S. B. Sitkin, L. B. Cardinal, & K. Bijlsma-Frankema (Eds.), *Organizational control* (pp. 51–79). Cambridge University Press.

Chakraborty, S., Tomsett, R., Raghavendra, R., Harborne, D., Alzantot, M., Cerutti, F., … Rao, R. M. (2017). *Interpretability of deep learning models: A survey of results.* Paper presented at the 2017 IEEE SmartWorld, Ubiquitous Intelligence & Computing, Advanced & Trusted Computed, Scalable Computing & Communications, Cloud & Big Data Computing, Internet of People and Smart City Innovation (SmartWorld/SCALCOM/UIC/ATC/CBDCom/IOP/SCI).

Copeland, R., & Hope, B. (2016). The world's largest hedge fund is building an algorithmic model from its employees' brains. *The Wall Street Journal.*

Falk, A., & Kosfeld, M. (2006). The hidden costs of control. *American Economic Review, 96*(5), 1611–1630.

Feldman, M. S. (2000). Organizational routines as a source of continuous change. *Organization Science, 11*(6), 611–629.

Fulmer, C. A., & Gelfand, M. J. (2012). At what level (and in whom) we trust: Trust across multiple organizational levels. *Journal of Management, 38*(4), 1167–1230.

Gillespie, N., Fulmer, C. A., & Lewicki, R. J. (Eds.). (2021). *Understanding trust in organizations: A multilevel perspective*. Routledge.

Gloor, P., Fischbach, K., Gluesing, J., Riopelle, K., & Schoder, D. (2018). Creating the collective mind through virtual mirroring based learning. *Development and Learning in Organizations: An International Journal, 32*(3), 4–7.

Hunkenschroer, A. L., & Luetge, C. (2022). Ethics of AI-enabled recruiting and selection: A review and research agenda. *Journal of Business Ethics*, 1–31.

Jordan, M. I., & Mitchell, T. M. (2015). Machine learning: Trends, perspectives, and prospects. *Science, 349*(6245), 255–260.

Lewis, J. D., & Weigert, A. (1985). Trust as a social reality. *Social Forces, 63*(4), 967–985.

Lewis, J. D., & Weigert, A. J. (2012). The social dynamics of trust: Theoretical and empirical research, 1985–2012. *Social Forces, 91*(1), 25–31.

Lockey, S., Gillespie, N., Holm, D., & Someh, I. A. (2021, January). A review of trust in AL: Challenges, vulnerabilities and future directions. In *Proceedings of the 54th Hawaii International Conference on System Sciences* (p. 5463).

Long, C. P., & Sitkin, S. B. (2018). Control–trust dynamics in organizations: Identifying shared perspectives and charting conceptual fault lines. *Academy of Management Annals, 12*(2), 725–751.

Love, E. G., & Kraatz, M. (2009). Character, conformity, or the bottom line? How and why downsizing affected corporate reputation. *Academy of Management Journal, 52*(2), 314–335.

Lynn, T., van der Werff, L., & Fox, G. (2021). Understanding trust and cloud computing: An integrated framework for assurance and accountability in the cloud. In *Data privacy and trust in cloud computing* (pp. 1–20). Palgrave Macmillan.

Mayer, R. C., Davis, J. H., & Schoorman, F. D. (1995). An integrative model of organizational trust. *Academy of Management Review, 20*(3), 709–734.

McKnight, D. H., Cummings, L. L., & Chervany, N. L. (1998). Initial trust formation in new organizational relationships. *Academy of Management Review, 23*(3), 473–490.

Meckel, M. (2018). *Mein Kopf gehört mir: Eine Reise durch die schöne neue Welt des Brainhacking*. Piper.

Mishina, Y., Block, E. S., & Mannor, M. J. (2012). The path dependence of organizational reputation: How social judgment influences assessments of capability and character. *Strategic Management Journal, 33*(5), 459–477.

Murray, A., Rhymer, J., & Sirmon, D. G. (2021). Humans and technology: Forms of conjoined agency in organizations. *Academy of Management Review, 46*(3), 552–571.

Nilsson, N. J. (2014). *Principles of AL.* Morgan Kaufmann Publishers.

Orlikowski, W. J., & Scott, S. V. (2014). What happens when evaluation goes online? Exploring apparatuses of valuation in the travel sector. *Organization Science, 25*, 868–891.

Petre, J. (2018). Big Brother is watching loo: Fears over 'smart' lavatory that can test users for drugs, pregnancy and urine problems. *Daily Mail on Sunday.* Retrieved September 1, 2022, from https://www.dailymail.co.uk/news/article-5905047/Fears-smart-lavatory-test-users-drugs-pregnancyurine-problems.html

Ravid, D. M., Tomczak, D. L., White, J. C., & Behrend, T. S. (2020). EPM 20/20: A review, framework, and research agenda for electronic performance monitoring. *Journal of Management, 46*(1), 100–126.

Schafheitle, S., Weibel, A., Ebert, I., Kasper, G., Schank, C., & Leicht-Deobald, U. (2020). No stone left unturned? Towards a framework for the impact of datafication technologies on organizational control. *Academy of Management Discoveries, 6*(3), 455–487.

Schafheitle, S., Weibel, A., & Rickert, A. (2021). The Bermuda Triangle of leadership in the AI era? Emerging trust implications from "two-leader-situations" in the eyes of employees. In *Proceedings of the 54th Hawaii International Conference on System Sciences* (pp. 5473–5482).

Schneider, P., & Sting, F. J. (2020). Employees' perspectives on digitalization-induced change: Exploring frames of industry 4.0. *Academy of Management Discoveries, 6*(3), 406–435.

Simpson, J. A. (2007). Psychological foundations of trust. *Current Directions in Psychological Science, 16*(5), 264–268.

Stanton, J. M., & Stam, K. R. (2006). *The visible employee: Using workplace monitoring and surveillance to protect information assets—Without compromising employee privacy or trust.* Information Today, Inc.

Stieglitz, S., Mirbabaie, M., Möllmann, N. R., & Rzyski, J. (2021). Collaborating with virtual assistants in organizations: Analyzing social loafing tendencies and responsibility attribution. *Information Systems Frontiers.*

Stone, M., Knapper, J., Evans, G., & Aravopoulou, E. (2018). Information management in the smart city. *The Bottom Line.*

Van den Heuvel, S., & Bondarouk, T. (2017). The rise (and fall?) of HR analytics: A study into the future application, value, structure, and system support. *Journal of Organizational Effectiveness: People and Performance, 4*(2), 157–178.

van der Werff, L., Blomqvist, K., & Koskinen, S. (2021). Trust cues in Artificial Intelligence. In *Understanding trust in organizations: A multilevel perspective.* Routledge.

von Krogh, G. (2018). Artificial Intelligence in organizations: New opportunities for phenomenon-based theorizing. *Academy of Management Discoveries, 4*(4), 404–409.

Wang, A. X., & MacLellan, L. (2018). Herman Miller's new Aeron chair is an office spy, collecting data on your every move. *Quartz Work*. Retrieved September 1, 2022, from https://qz.com/work/1218346/herman-millers-new-aeron-chair-isan-office-spy-collecting-data-on-your-every-move/

Weibel, A., den Hartog, D. N., Gillespie, N., Searle, R., Six, F., & Skinner, D. (2016). How do controls impact employee trust in the employer? *Human Resource Management, 55*(3), 437–462.

Whitener, E. M., Brodt, S. E., Korsgaard, M. A., & Werner, J. M. (1998). Managers as initiators of trust: An exchange relationship framework for understanding managerial trustworthy behavior. *Academy of Management Review, 23*(3), 513–530.

Zirkle, B., & Staples, W. (2005). Negotiating workplace surveillance. In J. Weckert (Ed.), *Electronic monitoring in the workplace: Controversies and solutions* (pp. 79–100). Idea Group Publishing.

CHAPTER 6

Leadership in Digitised Workplaces

Matej Černe, Amadeja Lamovšek, Irina Nikolova, and Sut I. Wong

Abstract Leadership represents an emerging theme in the field of digitised workplaces, yet the understanding of leadership dynamics and effectiveness in this context remains limited. The aim of this chapter is to (1) provide an overview of the existing academic literature at the intersection of leadership and the future of work and (2) propose an integrative framework of established and current research and emerging trends. We apply a holistic, systematic and comprehensive review of this literature based on objective measures of impact. We consider the main theoretical foundations within the literature and provide an overview of prominent research clusters including both current and emerging themes. Practical

M. Černe (✉) • A. Lamovšek
School of Economics and Business, University of Ljubljana, Ljubljana, Slovenia
e-mail: matej.cerne@ef.uni-lj.si; amadeja.lamovsek@ef.uni-lj.si

I. Nikolova
Maastricht University, Maastricht, The Netherlands
e-mail: i.nikolova@maastrichtuniversity.nl

S. I. Wong
BI Norwegian Business School, Oslo, Norway

T. Lynn et al. (eds.), *The Future of Work*, Palgrave Studies in Digital Business & Enabling Technologies,
https://doi.org/10.1007/978-3-031-31494-0_6

implications are related to leadership and digitalisation, leadership in virtual work, leading virtual teams and leadership in the context of the Future of Work and the gig economy.

Keywords Leadership • Digitised workplace literature review • Integrative framework

6.1 Introduction

Digitised workplaces, defined as workplaces in which digital technologies cause significant changes to a wide range of work processes and social relationships (Meske & Junglas, 2021), increasingly give rise to discussions around their possible implications for relationships, social ties, connectedness, communication and trust (Berg et al., 2018; Codagnone et al., 2016; Howcroft & Bergvall-Kåreborn, 2018; Kittur et al., 2013). To cultivate a connected environment in digitised workplaces with reduced physical interactions, questions regarding the role of leadership arise (Banks et al., 2022). According to a recent bibliometric review on the future of work (Santana & Cobo, 2020), leadership in the digitised workplace is a prevalent research theme that is emerging on the topic. However, understanding about leadership dynamics and effectiveness in this context remains limited. This is unfortunate as leaders possess important qualities that can act as crucial elements within employees' social contexts by providing instruction and feedback, but also support, guidance and motivation. These in turn can foster beneficial outcomes such as engagement, performance and creativity (Bartsch et al., 2020; Busse & Weidner, 2020; Liang et al., 2021).

The aim of this chapter is to (1) provide an overview of the existing academic literature at the intersection of leadership and the future of work, and (2) propose an integrative framework of established and current research and emerging trends. To do so, we conduct a systematic and bibliometric review[1] of the academic literature at the intersection between leadership and the future of work.

[1] Our systematic review leverages co-citation, co-word and bibliographic coupling analyses. For more details on bibliometric analysis and procedure and on the methodological background, see Zupic and Čater (2015) and van Eck and Waltman (2010), respectively. Detailed information on the literature search, applied thresholds and other methodological decisions, as well as results/clustering, is available from the authors upon request.

We identify the main theoretical foundations within this literature, current trends and emerging topics to propose a holistic review of prominent research clusters and their managerial implications. The chapter has a practical focus on the role of leadership, particularly in the context of digitally mediated work. Our selection of the most relevant areas is evidence-based and founded on objective measures of impact using bibliometric techniques. Our recommendations for practice refer to a range of leadership challenges and consider the ways in which these can be addressed in future work generally and in digitally mediated work specifically.

The remainder of this chapter is structured as follows. The next section presents an integrative framework of leadership in digitised workplaces that stems from our review. The following section provides an integrative framework of leadership in digitised workplaces. This is followed by a summary of topics that are gaining momentum in the literature and corresponding avenues for future research. The final section provides some concluding remarks.

6.2 Integrative Framework of Leadership in Digitised Workplaces

The theoretical foundations of research on leadership in the changing workplace focus primarily on leadership styles and approaches, trust (and the establishment of psychological safety) in the digital context, digital leadership (styles and approaches best suited to be communicated via digital means), global and distributed teams and consequences of digital work.

The current state-of-the-art of the field, derived from authors' keywords, is represented by topics of leadership and digitalisation, and leadership of virtual work (both focusing on leader–follower computer-mediated communication), virtual/distributed teams, and the future of work and gig economy (including self-leadership, stress-management and creativity).

Popular trends include leading virtual (team)work (computer-mediated communication and synergy and group interdependence), leader–follower relationship management (trust, emotional labour and psychological empowerment) and leadership capabilities in relation to various aspects of the gig economy[2] (management of collective competencies, globalisation, flexibilisation, social distancing, isolation, occupational safety and

[2] See Chap. 4 for a more detailed discussion.

organisational health in precarious work and more recently in light of the Covid-19 pandemic).

A comprehensive integrative framework of leadership in digital workplaces, derived from the bibliometric review, is portrayed in Fig. 6.1. It provides a synthesised summary of the clusters identified by the three bibliometric analyses, mirroring the split into three sections: fundamental, current and emerging themes. These serve as the basis for our discussion on the implications related to the best practice of leadership in the context of future work.

6.3 Implications: The Best Practice of Leadership in Digitised Workplaces

This section summarises some best practices for leaders in digitised workplaces that emerged from our review of the literature, specifically from the current themes identified in the studied field.

6.3.1 *Leadership and Digitalisation*

One of the most important leadership characteristics in the context of digitised workplaces is a leader's social presence, which refers to the psychological sense of being with others in the digital environment (Sivunen & Nordbäck, 2015). It represents an important variable that sheds light on leadership effectiveness in digitally mediated work. This presence consists of three dimensions: co-presence, behavioural engagement and psychological involvement (Biocca et al., 2001).

It is likely that different digital communication tools with various degrees of media richness can facilitate the different dimensions of leaders' social presence. Different communication technologies provide distinct degrees of informational value (Andres, 2002). In particular, text-based mass media with high convergence of information can, for instance, help to increase leaders' behavioural engagement. Richer media, such as video conferencing with highly synchronised communication, can help increase leaders' co-presence and psychological involvement by requiring more complex dialogue. As such, leaders should be mindful of the dynamics of various media to best utilise these tools to increase their social presence, which in turn will enable them to initiate and develop relationships and social connections in their organisations.

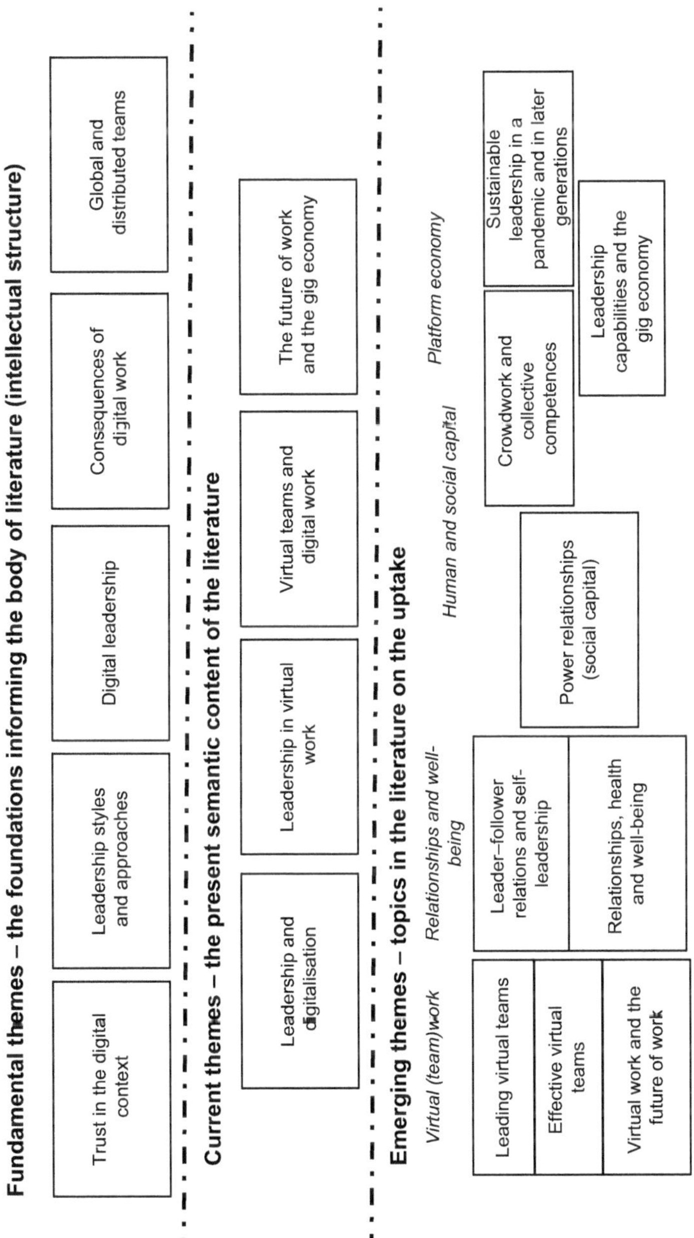

Fig. 6.1 Integrative framework of leadership in digitised workplaces

Trust represents a crucial outcome of high-quality work relationships. Building trust and psychological safety inside digital environments is more difficult because virtual teams tend to be more task-oriented and rely on already-established relationships (Liao, 2017). To develop relationships among virtual teams, which are the foundation of trust, leaders should establish early face-to-face meetings, as well as frequent meetings using media-rich communication channels (Maznevski & Chudoba, 2000). In addition, leadership that is aimed at fostering trust in digital environments should focus on creating clarity about team norms, managing team expectations and allowing members to connect through shared experiences on a regular basis. Given that some of the cues that help individuals appraise and make sense of their environment during face-to-face communication (i.e., non-verbal communication) are obscured during digital communication, virtual team members are particularly reliant on apparent transparency to build inter-team trust (Jarvenpaa et al., 1997).

6.3.2 *Leadership in Virtual Work*

A reduced sense of leaders' co-presence that is inherent in digital workplaces can also affect certain leadership approaches. For instance, some evidence suggests that transformational leadership can be less effective in teams that are highly virtual (Wong & Berntzen, 2019). This would suggest that leadership influences can be filtered out in digitally mediated environments and certain leadership cues and communications may fail to be translated and/or adequately utilised via different digital media, especially when different forms of work (on-site, hybrid, off-site) are used interchangeably.

As the move towards more virtual work can be taxing on individuals' adaptability and mental health, it is not fully known how they can affect the well-being and functioning of the focal employee and the team (Nikolova et al., 2014). Leadership styles and behaviours (e.g., servant, engaging or ethical leadership, and leaders' adaptable capacities such as a need for structure) that are thought to promote well-being and adaptability in traditional office environments (Chughtai et al., 2015; Kaltiainen & Hakanen, 2020; Okpozo et al., 2017) might be helpful for employees coping with frequent and swift changes from non-digital to fully digital work (and vice versa).

6.3.3 *Leading Virtual Teams and Digital Work*

Similar concerns are also imposed on virtual team coordination. Recent research from the perspective of Media Synchronicity Theory (MST) suggests that teams can communicate effectively or poorly regardless of the media used (e.g., Hassell & Limayem, 2017). MST suggests an orchestrated use of media where team members' ways of communicating and coordinating correspond with each other (Dennis et al., 2008). Indeed, the team's ability to coordinate might be influenced more by the harmonised use of media among team members than by the richness of the media used. In virtual work, however, opportunities for physical social contact are limited, which can negatively influence a team's ability to coordinate effectively (Kreijns et al., 2007).

A shared understanding of how communication should be carried out is therefore especially crucial to the coordination of virtual teams (e.g., Müller & Antoni, 2020). This parallels with more recent research on digital communication, where the way in which these different media are being used in teams matters (Gilson et al., 2015). This may include providing digital workers with charismatic video messages which can help in conveying leadership tactics (Nieken, 2022) though leaders need to be careful not to send messages that are too simple or too subtle and therefore not explicit enough (Fest et al., 2021).

6.3.4 *Leadership in the Context of the Future of Work and Gig Economy*

Besides more traditional types of employment, new forms of labour, such as platform gig work, have emerged in the 'digital economy' and have increasingly replaced fixed employer–employee relationships with new, flexible structures (Gandini, 2018; Prassl & Risak, 2016). The precarious working environments of platform or gig workers are well recognised and are characterised by high levels of job insecurity and a lack of job and career development (Wong et al., 2021).

Recent studies point to the importance of workers' resilience and proactivity to gig workers' active improvement of better job security and working conditions. To stimulate these attributes, leaders can assist gig workers in identifying opportunities, planning and pursuing goals, providing training on building self-confidence, self-regulation and self-efficacy (Bateman & Crant, 1999). Leaders can also encourage gig workers to be more proactive and resilient by shaping the work environment to provide more social support (Ghitulescu, 2012; Thomas Hendricks & Albright, 2018). In the context of gig work, the availability of communication channels influences followers' expectations about appropriate leader communication, meaning that the lack of non-verbal cues might not matter too much in a pure online setting (Fest et al., 2021).

6.4 Future Research Directions of Leadership in the Context of the Future of Work

Based on the topics that are emerging in the literature, we have identified several avenues that would benefit from additional research.

6.4.1 *Virtual Work and Virtual Teamwork*

Communication technologies that enable digital work designs, such as virtual teams, are disrupting organisation design and work processes (Gilson et al., 2015) and will continue to do so in the future. Research consistently shows that virtual teams can be more challenging to lead than face-to-face teams, creating new demands for leaders (Gibson & Cohen, 2003). Due to teams' reduced physical presence, relationship development and the establishment of social connections is considered one of the most important competencies required for leaders to reinforce and maintain effective team processes (Liao, 2017). The importance of this leadership skill is not new (Cropanzano et al., 2017). What is new and in much need of future research, however, is how leaders can build relationships and social connections via digital means.

Communication processes act as links between individuals, whose collaborative interactions create a shared social identity (Jeong & Chi, 2007; Kane et al., 2005). It is, however, unclear how team dynamics in terms of using different media affect the shared understanding of the task and the team, and thus the team's virtual coordination. Future research into the effects of media configuration within teams could therefore be fruitful.

6.4.2 *Leader–Follower Relationships, Health and Well-being*

Another topic that has attracted research attention in the past and is still worth further exploration concerns leadership approaches to fostering trust and managing stress in the digital environment. With advances in information technology and—due to the recent Covid-19 pandemic—restrictions on traditional office work, many leaders have been faced with the question of how to lead virtual teams, to build or maintain a team's trust (in its leader or among employees), and to manage the increase in stress and strain among employees. Compared to traditional face-to-face leadership, digital leadership—like team dynamics—is more challenging in digital settings (Carte et al., 2006).

While the accumulated knowledge thus far provides some insight into which tools and approaches leaders can use to nurture trusting relationships with and among team members in virtual settings, an apparent gap in the literature is the lack of understanding of how leaders should act in a dynamic environment, where the degree of team virtuality changes frequently. Early face-to-face meetings among team members are advisable for building trust in a new team, but there is a lack of evidence on how to achieve this when a new team has no opportunity for face-to-face interactions or when new members join a team, but face-to-face meetings are no longer an option. Successful integration of such newcomers and building their trust is crucial to their well-being and functioning, as well as to that of their team. Further research is needed to guide leaders in helping newcomers develop trusting relationships with their teams in dynamic virtual settings.

In response to the recent Covid-19 pandemic, considerable research attention has been directed at exploring the effect of digital work on work stress (Bregenzer & Jimenez, 2021; González-Anta et al., 2021). Despite initial evidence on leadership behaviours (e.g., health-promoting leadership) that can buffer the harmful effects of digital work on employees' well-being, it is necessary to accumulate more knowledge on leaders' behaviours and their approaches to leading teams in contexts with fluctuating degrees of virtuality (from highly physical to highly virtual).

6.4.3 *Human Capital, Social Capital and Leadership of Networks*

Differences in the choice of communication media might be a function of individual needs and regulatory mechanisms such as the need for connectedness (Richardson & Benbunan-Fich, 2011). During the first two years of the pandemic, restrictions for many digital workers meant an increase in isolation and loneliness (Andel et al., 2021).[3] In general, digital workers have limited opportunities to have spontaneous interactions with colleagues (e.g., small talk by the coffee machine), which might mean that some individuals, in order to cope with loneliness and isolation (especially as their social contacts outside of work are also limited), might prefer using media-rich communication channels with colleagues, and especially supervisors. Future studies might explore social networks (e.g., friendly, helping, formal and informal work connections) and individual connectedness (e.g., network position, status, centrality) as a predictor of media channel preference, and the role of leaders in constructing and maintaining the structure of those networks.

In addition to team process characteristics, leadership styles and personal differences, cultural differences might play a role in employees' choice and use of communication media. Prior research has shown that cultural diversity plays a role in the selection of communication media (Shachaf, 2008). The results of an exploratory, interview-based study (Klitmøller & Lauring, 2013) suggest that in addition to the types of knowledge that need to be shared, the cultural and linguistic variations between the communicating parties (i.e., leaders and followers) influence the choice of media. Future studies might conduct a cross-cultural comparative analysis investigating how communication media channels are used by leaders across cultures and how cultural differences might affect communication effectiveness and team coordination in virtual settings.

6.4.4 Leadership in the Platform-Mediated Economy

With the increase in popularity of digital platforms, it is important to recognise that platform organisations can foster more supportive and collaborative platform environments to help gig workers connect and find support. A fruitful future research avenue would be the investigation of the role of platform interface and algorithmic design in facilitating collaborative online communities to enhance gig worker participation. Leaders have a limited role on gig platforms due to the lack of social interactions, but the elements of leadership, such as framing requests and providing appropriate feedback (Wong et al., 2021) or motivating 'nudges' (Fest et al., 2021), need to be carefully incorporated into algorithmic communication to develop gig workers' performance.

[3] See Chap. 2 for a more detailed discussion.

Another form of leadership that might be emerging and that could play a key role to the platform-mediated team interactions is machine or Artificial Intelligence (AI)-based leadership. Despite initial evidence regarding its wide applicability and usefulness, as well as the limitations of such AI leadership or AI coaching (Parent-Rocheleau & Parker, 2021), using AI as a servant leader or moderator in online communities, as well as determining which leadership styles would be best suited (for AI-based leadership) to apply in different situations, remains an uncharted territory. Future studies might also focus on testing the link between AI situational and adaptable leadership reflecting the ability of AI to adapt its leadership style depending on the situation and the individual characteristics of the employee.

6.5 Conclusion

It is apparent that digital technologies have had, and will continue to have, substantial impact on how business is (and will be) operated and how work is (and will be) carried out. Constant and often drastic changes require high levels of adaptability from organisations and their leaders. In such a fast-paced, ever-changing environment, trust and psychological safety consistently stand out as crucial for employees to adapt and thrive in the change process. To foster sustainable digital work environments and leadership, it is recommended that organisations and leaders pay attention to not only what digital technologies should be used but also how these are used to achieve their goals.

Acknowledgement This work was supported by the Slovenian research agency (Core project funding J5-2555 and P5-0441).

References

Andel, S. A., Shen, W., & Arvan, M. L. (2021). Depending on your own kindness: The moderating role of self-compassion on the within-person consequences of work loneliness during the COVID-19 pandemic. *Journal of Occupational Health Psychology, 26*(4), 276–290.

Andres, H. P. (2002). A comparison of face-to-face and virtual software development teams. *Team Performance Management, 8*(1/2), 39–48.

Banks, G. C., Dionne, S. D., Mast, M. S., & Sayama, H. (2022). Leadership in the digital era: A review of who, what, when, where, and why. *The Leadership Quarterly, 101634.*

Bartsch, S., Weber, E., Büttgen, M., & Huber, A. (2020). Leadership matters in crisis-induced digital transformation: How to lead service employees effectively during the COVID-19 pandemic. *Journal of Service Management, 32*(1), 71–85.

Bateman, T., & Crant, M. (1999). Proactive behavior: Meaning, impact, recommendations. *Business Horizons, 42*(3), 63–74.

Berg, J., Furrer, M., Harmon, E., Rani, U., & Silberman, S. M. (2018). Digital labour platforms and the future of work towards decent work in the online world. *International Labour Office.*

Biocca, F., Harms, C., & Gregg, J. L. (2001). *The networked minds measure of social presence: Pilot test of the factor structure and concurrent validity.* 4th Annual International Workshop on Presence.

Bregenzer, A., & Jimenez, P. (2021). Risk factors and leadership in a digitalized working world and their effects on employees' stress and resources: Web-based questionnaire study. *Journal of Medical Internet Research, 23*(3).

Busse, R., & Weidner, G. (2020). A qualitative investigation on combined effects of distant leadership, organisational agility and digital collaboration on perceived employee engagement. *Leadership and Organization Development Journal, 41*(4), 535–550.

Carte, T. A., Chidambaram, L., & Becker, A. (2006). Emergent leadership in self-managed virtual teams: A longitudinal study of concentrated and shared leadership behaviors. *Group Decision and Negotiation, 15*(4), 323–343.

Chughtai, A., Byrne, M., & Flood, B. (2015). Linking ethical leadership to employee well-being: The role of trust in supervisor. *Journal of Business Ethics, 128*(3), 653–663.

Codagnone, C., Abadie, F., & Biagi, F. (2016). *The future of work in the "sharing economy".*

Cropanzano, R., Anthony, E. L., Daniels, S. R., & Hall, A. V. (2017). Social exchange theory: A critical review with theoretical remedies. *Academy of Management Annals, 11*(1), 479–516.

Dennis, A. R., Fuller, R. M., & Valacich, J. S. (2008). Media, tasks, and communication processes: A theory of media synchronicity. *MIS Quarterly: Management Information Systems, 32*(3), 575–600.

Fest, S., Kvaløy, O., Nieken, P., & Schöttner, A. (2021). How (not) to motivate online workers: Two controlled field experiments on leadership in the gig economy. *The Leadership Quarterly, 32*(6).

Gandini, A. (2018). Labour process theory and the gig economy. *Human Relations, 72*(6), 1039–1056.

Ghitulescu, B. E. (2012). Making change happen: The impact of work context on adaptive and proactive behaviors. *The Journal of Applied Behavioral Science, 49*(2), 206–245.

Gibson, C., & Cohen, S. G. (2003). *Virtual teams that work: Creating conditions for virtual team effectiveness.* Jossey-Bass.

Gilson, L. L., Maynard, M. T., Young, N. C. J., Vartiainen, M., & Hakonen, M. (2015). Virtual teams research: 10 years, 10 themes, and 10 opportunities. *Journal of Management, 41*(5), 1313–1337.

González-Anta, B., Orengo, V., Zornoza, A., Peñarroja, V., & Gamero, N. (2021). Sustainable virtual teams: Promoting well-being through affect management training and openness to experience configurations. *Sustainability, 13*(6), 3491.

Hassell, M. D., & Limayem, M. (2017). Media impacts and performance in dispersed teams. *Journal of Computer Information Systems, 60*(1), 18–25.

Howcroft, D., & Bergvall-Kåreborn, B. (2018). A typology of crowdwork platforms. *Work, Employment and Society, 33*(1), 21–38.

Jarvenpaa, S. L., Knoll, K., & Leidner, D. E. (1997). Is anybody out there? Antecedents of trust in global virtual teams. *Journal of Management Information Systems, 14*(4), 29–64.

Jeong, H., & Chi, T. H. (2007). Knowledge convergence and collaborative learning. *Instructional Science*, 287–315.

Kaltiainen, J., & Hakanen, J. (2020). Fostering task and adaptive performance through employee well-being: The role of servant leadership. *BRQ Business Research Quarterly.*

Kane, A. A., Argote, L., & Levine, J. M. (2005). Knowledge transfer between groups via personnel rotation: Effects of social identity and knowledge quality. *Organizational Behavior and Human Decision Processes, 96*(1), 56–71.

Kittur, A., Nickerson, J. V., Bernstein, M. S., Gerber, E. M., Shaw, A., Zimmerman, J., Lease, M., & Horton, J. J. (2013). *The future of crowd work.* Proceedings of the ACM Conference on Computer Supported Cooperative Work, CSCW, 1301–1317.

Klitmøller, A., & Lauring, J. (2013). When global virtual teams share knowledge: Media richness, cultural difference and language commonality. *Journal of World Business, 48*(3), 398–406.

Kreijns, K., Kirschner, P. A., Jochems, W., & van Buuren, H. (2007). Measuring perceived sociability of computer-supported collaborative learning environments. *Computers & Education, 49*(2), 176–192.

Liang, B., van Knippenberg, D., & Gu, Q. (2021). A cross-level model of shared leadership, meaning, and individual creativity. *Journal of Organizational Behavior, 42*(1), 68–83.

Liao, C. (2017). Leadership in virtual teams: A multilevel perspective. *Human Resource Management Review, 27*(4), 648–659.

Maznevski, M. L., & Chudoba, K. M. (2000). Bridging space over time: Global virtual team dynamics and effectiveness. *Organization Science, 11*(5), 473–492.

Meske, C., & Junglas, I. (2021). Investigating the elicitation of employees' support towards digital workplace transformation. *Behaviour & Information Technology, 40*(11), 1120–1136.

Müller, R., & Antoni, C. H. (2020). Individual perceptions of shared mental models of information and communication technology (ICT) and virtual team coordination and performance-the moderating role of flexibility in ICT use. *Group Dynamics, 24*(3), 186–200.

Nieken, P. (2022). Charisma in the gig economy: The impact of digital leadership and communication channels on performance. *The Leadership Quarterly, 101631.*

Nikolova, I., van Ruysseveldt, J., de Witte, H., & Syroit, J. (2014). Well-being in times of task restructuring: The buffering potential of workplace learning. *Work and Stress, 28*(3), 217–235.

Okpozo, A. Z., Gong, T., Ennis, M. C., & Adenuga, B. (2017). Investigating the impact of ethical leadership on aspects of burnout. *Leadership and Organization Development Journal, 38*(8), 1128–1143.

Parent-Rocheleau, X., & Parker, S. K. (2021). Algorithms as work designers: How algorithmic management influences the design: How algorithmic management influences the design of jobs. *Human Resource Management Review*, 100838.

Prassl, J. F. B., & Risak, M. (2016). Uber, TaskRabbit and Co: Platforms as employers? Rethinking the legal analysis of crowdwork. *Comparative Labor Law and Policy Journal, 37*(3), 619–652.

Richardson, K., & Benbunan-Fich, R. (2011). Examining the antecedents of work connectivity behavior during non-work time. *Information and Organization, 21*(3), 142–160.

Santana, M., & Cobo, M. J. (2020). What is the future of work? A science mapping analysis. *European Management Journal, 38*(6), 846–862.

Shachaf, P. (2008). Cultural diversity and information and communication technology impacts on global virtual teams: An exploratory study. *Information and Management, 45*(2), 131–142.

Sivunen, A., & Nordbäck, E. (2015). Social presence as a multi-dimensional group construct in 3D virtual environments. *Journal of Computer-Mediated Communication, 20*(1), 19–36.

Thomas Hendricks, K., & Albright, D. (2018). The theory and practice of training resilience. In K. Thomas Hendricks & D. Albright (Eds.), *Bulletproofing the psyche: Preventing mental health problems in our military and veterans* (pp. 69–75). ABC-CLIO.

van Eck, N. J., & Waltman, L. (2010). Software survey: VOSviewer, a computer program for bibliometric mapping. *Scientometrics, 84*(2), 523–538.

Wong, S. I., & Berntzen, M. N. (2019). Transformational leadership and leader–member exchange in distributed teams: The roles of electronic dependence and team task interdependence. *Computers in Human Behavior, 92*, 381–392.

Wong, S. I., Bunjak, A., Černe, M., & Fieseler, C. (2021). Fostering creative performance of platform crowdworkers: The digital feedback dilemma. *International Journal of Electronic Commerce, 25*(3), 263–286.

Zupic, I., & Čater, T. (2015). Bibliometric methods in management and organization. *Organizational Research Methods, 18*(3), 429–472.

CHAPTER 7

Diversity and Inclusion

Jean McCarthy, Janine Bosak, Jeanette N. Cleveland, and Emma Parry

Abstract The composition of the workforce, the pool of potential job applicants, and the diversity of the workplace are changing. In this chapter, we focus on the future of workplace diversity and inclusion of human workers, as well as how diversity and inclusion are likely to be affected by developments in technology (e.g., artificial intelligence and non-human presence at work). We argue that these technological developments are likely to have an

J. McCarthy (✉)
Kemmy Business School, University of Limerick, Limerick, Ireland
e-mail: jean.mccarthy@ul.ie

J. Bosak
DCU Business School, Dublin City University, Dublin, Ireland
e-mail: janine.bosak@dcu.ie

J. N. Cleveland
Department of Psychology, Colorado State University, Fort Collins, CO, USA
e-mail: jncl0@icloud.com

E. Parry
Cranfield School of Management, Cranfield University, Bedfordshire, UK
e-mail: emma.parry@cranfield.ac.uk

T. Lynn et al. (eds.), *The Future of Work*, Palgrave Studies in Digital Business & Enabling Technologies,
https://doi.org/10.1007/978-3-031-31494-0_7

impact on how organisations react to the increasing diversity of the workforce, and that they have the potential to either enhance or impede diversity and inclusion. We consider the implications of increasing diversity for organisations, such as changes to legal and economic structures, reimagining work-family balance and working time, the use of technology in reducing bias and, importantly, a focus on organisational cultures and individual attitudes that might promote a more diverse, inclusive and, indeed, sustainable workplace in the years ahead.

Keywords Diversity • Inclusion • Attitudes • Stereotypes • Bias • Decision-making • Social roles • Technology • Organisational culture

7.1 Introduction

Workplace diversity suggests that employees and managers, as well as suppliers, clients and customers, are different in several ways, including, *inter alia*, their gender, race, age, ethnicity, health, disability, sexual orientation, nationality, language, religion, caring responsibilities, education and previous career experience. The composition of the workforce, the pool of potential job applicants and the diversity of the workplace are changing. In the last two years, the Covid-19 pandemic has reduced the participation of both older workers and women in the workforce (Stevenson, 2021), but longer-term trends suggest that the workforce will become increasingly diverse in terms of race, ethnicity, gender, age, religion, culture, nationality and language. At the same time, technological advances beyond automation, such as artificial intelligence (AI), cloud computing, and social media, have significantly permeated both our work and non-work lives, and these changes have the potential to accelerate the diversification of the workforce. Consequently, workforces and many workplaces across the globe no longer have a dominant, traditional or homogenous pool of workers, nor do they have universal structures or approaches to work and working time.

This increasing workplace diversity has implications for many aspects of the Future of Work in organisations, starting with the way that work is organised. In particular, the combination of human and non-human interactions and job/occupational task redistributions is likely to change over time, based upon yet-to-be articulated criteria of what humans/non-human can perform best. Technological changes have significant potential to change outcomes such as organisational profits, worker health, and the nature of human-based jobs and non-human centred work, influencing the relative balance of worker and organisational influences on these outcomes (Ozkazanc-Pan, 2021). To develop and maintain the sustainability of organisations for human workers, organisational decision-makers need to structure work systems, practices, emerging technology and the cultures of organisations, to adapt to this changing environment.

In this chapter, we focus upon the future of workplace diversity and inclusion of human workers, as well as how diversity and inclusion are likely to be affected by developments in technology (e.g., AI and non-human presence at work). Our discussion here centres on an understanding of diversity through a multi-level lens as a strategy for moving considerations of diversity and inclusion towards a broader framework for the future. Included in this is the multi-level lens is a recognition of the increasingly important role of technology and AI at all levels of workplace diversity and inclusion.

Human and non-human diversity is a nuanced and complex topic. Our examples throughout the chapter focus largely on gender, race and age issues, since we know that people automatically evaluate other people, at least in the first instance, along these three dimensions of diversity (Nelson, 2004). We will argue that developments in technology are likely to have an impact on how organisations react to the increasing diversity of the workforce and that they have the potential to either enhance or impede diversity and inclusion. Finally, we consider the implications of increasing diversity for organisations, with a focus on interventions and policies that might promote a more diverse, inclusive and indeed, sustainable workplace in the years ahead. We thus expect our chapter to generate reflective and critical discussions about the future of workplace diversity and inclusion.

7.2 Human Diversity and Inclusion Through a Multi-level Lens: Individual-Group and Institutional Levels

Often, theories of bias and prejudice, as well as programmes and interventions for reducing bias at work (e.g., unconscious bias training), assume that some subset of individuals hold negative views or stereotypes about people who are different from them, and more positive views about people who they view as similar. Generalised beliefs individuals have about members of specific groups in society are usually labelled as stereotypes, and these beliefs underlie much of the past research on diversity and inclusion. Stereotypes represent a "relatively simple cognition, especially of a social group" (Krech et al., 1962, p. 67), which is exaggerated in two important ways (Allport, 1954). First, all members of that group are seen as sharing a set of attributes, and second, beliefs or knowledge about these group attributes are used to make judgements about individuals. Prejudice encompasses an overall emotional feeling concerning an individual or group (Berkowitz, 2000), and these beliefs and feelings are thought to drive behaviours and actions towards these individuals or groups (Fazio, 1986, 1995). That is, individuals express their attitudes by means of holding certain beliefs about an individual or group (stereotypes), feeling a certain way about an individual or group (prejudice) and intending to behave in a certain way towards an individual or group (discrimination).

While individual beliefs and beliefs shared among group members are an important component of bias, prejudice and discrimination, these beliefs and assumptions can become institutionalised, and their effects can continue to be felt long after the individuals whose beliefs created these institutional norms, rules, regulations and laws have passed from the scene. It is therefore useful to consider both individual-group level explanations for bias, prejudice and discrimination and institutional explanations.

Individual and Group-Level Explanations. Stereotypes reflect people's consensual beliefs about groups of people including beliefs about the physical, personality and social characteristics of women and men, ethnic groups, age and generational groups, religions and so forth. By observing a given behaviour, an observer infers that the person possesses a given trait or characteristic. For example, one might observe a woman comforting a baby or an elderly person. An inference is made that women are nurturing and gentle. Further, these traits may be seen as stable across all members of that group with little variability: all women are nurturing or gentle. The study of group stereotypes emerged in psychology and sociological research on social role theory (Eagly, 1997). Social role theory has its origins in efforts to understand the perceptions of gender behaviour. Empirical findings have suggested that there is a wide variation in perceptions of gender differences and similarities across contexts (Eagly, 1987, 1997), but also suggest that perceivers have complex yet relatively stable sets of beliefs and associations concerning men and women (Eagly, 1997; Bosak et al., 2012).

For example, Eagly and Steffen's (1984) seminal work established that gender stereotypes can be explained by a consideration of women's and men's occupational roles. Men are often viewed in the role of "breadwinner" (or the employee of higher status), while women are often viewed in the role of homemaker (or employee of lower status). Women are therefore disproportionately represented in roles requiring communal traits, for example "concerned for the welfare of others" (Deaux & Kite, 1993, p. 113). Men are disproportionately represented in roles requiring agentic traits, for example assertiveness (Eagly, 1997). Observing women and men in these occupational roles leads people to associate the characteristics of these roles with the individuals who occupy them; therefore, people conclude that women are typically communal and men are typically agentic (Eagly & Steffen, 1984). Further, women may be directed largely towards these jobs rather than occupations that are associated with other traits or characteristics that may be associated with men (Acker, 1990), creating and reinforcing occupational sex segregation of jobs. This segregation of occupations by gender, race or age reinforces other's perceptions that some jobs are more suited for individuals based on their gender, race and age rather than based on *job-related* skills, knowledge or characteristics.

Individual-level explanations of bias and discrimination endure for a number of reasons. Most people can agree there are stereotypes and discrimination that can create barriers to diversity and inclusion. We can usually "see" or observe bias at an individual or even group level. For example, we might observe instances where one employee is treated differently from others, perhaps because of their gender or race. We might also track group differences in outcomes by recording decisions such as hiring, promotions or pay increases for individuals from diverse groups compared to a majority group. If we observe differences in the ways individuals or groups are treated in the workplace, we are likely to search for explanations that involve familiar concepts such as stereotypes, prejudice or discrimination. For example, when an employee habitually arrives late to virtual meetings, we may attribute this to individual factors (e.g., stereotype that person as lazy or undependable) or to group/demographic factors (e.g., stereotype that person as coming from a culture that does not place an emphasis on timeliness).

As we move to more organisational and institutional explanations, there is less agreement on discriminatory behaviours and practices as they are more difficult to clearly articulate or "see", often because such things are accepted as "normal". That is, we have built an entire series of institutions (e.g., legal systems, corporations) around the experience of the past several centuries, when work was largely the domain of one small subset of the population (generally, male members of the dominant racial/ethnic groups), and these institutions can often create subtle but powerful barriers to diversity and inclusion. These individual and group-level explanations for bias and discrimination are useful but insufficient; if we ignore broader societal factors, we are likely to arrive at a limited understanding of why diversity continues to be a challenge in work and organisations. One of the arguments in this chapter is that we must also consider structural and institutional factors. Returning to the example above that an individual is consistently late to virtual meetings, rather than applying a person-centred attribution or stereotype (e.g., person is lazy), it may be that this individual lives in a rural location that has slow internet connectivity. Our stereotype of laziness to the attributes of the individual (and in other instances, the attributes of groups) may mislead us if we ignore broader structural barriers to arriving on time to a virtual meeting.

Institutional-Level Explanations for Bias and Discrimination. There is a growing body of scholarship that examines phenomena such as racism and sexism (e.g., Acker, 2006) as a feature of organisations rather than simply the product of individual stereotypes and decisions. For example, Ray (2019) proposes that organisations are racial structures connecting organisational rules to social and material resources. Racial hierarchies in organisations enhance or diminish the agency of racial groups, legitimate the unequal distribution of resources and establish a set of norms for desired behaviours (e.g., whiteness is treated as a credential). More generally, organisations create norms and hierarchies that both put some people in advantaged positions (e.g., white middle-aged males) and that serve to justify those hierarchies by defining what is normal and expected (Acker, 1990, 2006). Thus, our beliefs about and perceptions of work and workers include "[…] a host of general organisational patterns, including gendered hierarchies, the division between paid work and unpaid housework, and the distinction between production and reproduction" (Ray, 2019, p. 32).

Diversity scholars (e.g., Davis, 1983) argue that many forms of racism and sexism can be best understood as ways of rationalising and naturalising existing racial and gender-based hierarchies. That is, the fact that work, especially work that involves power and status, has traditionally been the exclusive preserve of a subset of male workers, creates a norm that suggests to many that it *should* be the preserve of that subset and that workers from other strata of society should not strive for or occupy these positions.

Still others (Bowser, 2017) stress that any adequate theory of racism (or sexism, ageism—authors' addition) should include cultural, institutional and personal factors. For example, proponents of Critical Race Theory argue that racism is often embedded in and codified in social and legal structures (e.g., discriminatory practices in giving access to home ownership) that have the effect of maintaining existing racial hierarchies (George, 2021).

Beliefs about who should hold different types of jobs, positions or power, control over resources, etc., develop over time, and these do not necessarily require individual animus towards members of disadvantaged groups. Rather, these beliefs represent a set of assumptions about what is "normal", and they often lag rather than lead changes in society. This does suggest, however, that over time as the workforce changes, jobs that had traditionally been seen as reserved for one group of people (often, white middle-aged males) may in the future be seen as more open to a more diverse set of individuals.

As technology starts to change the nature of work and the skills required for work, it is possible that there will be changes in the content of stereotypes and their effects on workers and organisations. Age discrimination, for example, might increase, as jobs require the use of more complex technologies. There is evidence, for example, that older workers are seen as having more difficulty learning and adjusting to new technologies (Parry & McCarthy, 2017). Discrimination based on ethnicity, education or race, however, might decrease as technology takes over some of the skills once required. Delivery truck drivers, for example, once were required to make decisions about their routes, the order in which to serve customers and the way their vans were loaded, but many of these decisions now reside in route-planning software, arguably lowering the skill levels required of drivers (Kaiser-Schatzlein, 2022).

7.3 Implications for the Future of Work

Organisations often find it difficult to provide an inclusive work environment that gives a diverse workforce an opportunity to succeed, in large part because they were often built by and for a very different (more homogeneous) workforce. Individual-level theories of prejudice and discrimination (e.g., social role theory) are useful, but it is necessary to consider how organisational norms and cultures create barriers for a diverse workforce. The criteria that have traditionally defined individual and organisational success (e.g., profit, competition, advancement) also tend to support a particular pattern of hierarchy and advantage that may have been functional when the workforce was largely homogeneous and when discrimination was broadly accepted in society. As the workforce becomes more diverse, as people, and more specifically organisational decision-makers, become more aware of detrimental discriminatory attitudes and behaviour, and as technology radically transforms the nature of work, organisations have an opportunity to rethink their definition of what represents success and what individuals should do to help organisations succeed.

7.3.1 Legal and Economic Structures

Changes in attitudes towards disadvantaged groups can be slow, especially when these attitudes are enshrined in legal and economic structures (e.g., Jim Crow laws in the southern parts of the U.S.). This suggests that it is critically important to examine legal and economic structures that may stand in the way of progress. For example, in the U.S., women were substantially more likely to leave the workforce than men during the Covid pandemic, in part because of the distribution of males and females in jobs directly affected by the pandemic and in part because of the collapse of the childcare industry, itself mainly staffed by women (Stevenson, 2021). The differences in the experiences of male and female workers are in part related to perceptions of sex roles, but it is more broadly related to large-scale economic factors that are sometimes correlated with, but rarely determined solely by, role perceptions.

For example, with the growth of information technology and AI, a new economy has emerged that rests significantly on technology and boasts flexibility and autonomy to workers and is based on short-term, temporary and contract work, on-demand work relationships with companies (e.g., Uber, GrubHub).[1] Such technology shifts at work may have a stronger impact on disadvantaged workers (e.g., women, immigrants, members of racial and ethnic minority groups), in part because of differential access to reliable technologies and in part because of their concentration in relatively low-skilled jobs are more easily automated by technology.

[1] See Chap. 4 for a more detailed discussion.

7.3.2 Work-Family Balance and Working Time

The digital transformation and the fourth industrial revolution also require a work transformation for an increasingly digital economy and work environment, including a need for more agile work models—with radical shifts in when and where we work, which have been accelerated by the Covid-19 crisis (OECD, 2021). New working time patterns that embrace flexibility might be seen as more female-friendly (Howcroft & Rubery, 2019) because women might like to work flexibly and at home (Denham, 2018). However, the emerging work models also bear certain risks with, for example fragmented or discontinuous time leading to increased work intensity during paid hours (Rubery et al., 2015) or remote working contributing to work intensification (Kelliher & Anderson, 2010) and blurred boundaries between work, family and personal time (Kossek & Lautsch, 2012). Further the argument is made that flexible working might help women better manage the "double burden" of paid work and unpaid work at home (McKinsey Global Institute, 2019)—which however might further reinforce gender inequalities rather than reduce them.

7.3.3 Reducing Bias with Technology

Given the prevalence of stereotypes and their continuing influence in current societies, it appears critical to ensure that bias is not being built into technologies and systems, old and new, during the production stages—"reflecting the prejudices and blind spots of their creators and often reinforcing damaging societal norms" (Jivani, 2020, p. 139). Although digital platforms might make it easier for women to successfully navigate cultural barriers present in some countries in the formal economy (OECD, 2017), there are also examples of biased data going into systems, thus encoding the history of gender bias within digital platforms (Wajcman, 2018). A good example of this was Amazon's AI recruitment system which learned to downgrade resumes that mention "women" based on a decade of resume information from people applying for jobs at Amazon fed into the system.

7.3.4 Attitudes and Culture

There is a need for employers and managers to be attentive to the culture that exists in their workplace in relation to diversity and inclusion. The creation of "awareness" policies, practices and both synchronous and asynchronous training that challenge latent attitudes and prevent them from affecting discriminatory or exclusion behaviours is recommended. Astley and Cherkashyna (2021), for example, recommend the formalisation of a diversity development pipeline process in organisations encompassing mentoring and training/development support, as well as digital communication programmes, all focused on increasing minority representation—particularly female and Black, Asian and minority ethnic (BAME)—at the top of the organisation. It has to be communicated in practice that in an increasingly diverse society, the need to optimise the entire pool of workers has never been more critical and neither has challenging discriminatory attitudes and behaviours.

7.4 Conclusion

Technological developments now, and into the future, will have an impact on how organisations manage the increasing diversity of the workforce and the way in which work is organised. Organisations must provide an inclusive work environment that gives a diverse workforce an opportunity to succeed. To do this, it is necessary to consider how both nascent stereotypes and overt discrimination among organisational decision-makers can be reduced, and how barriers related to organisational norms and cultures can be deconstructed in the face of a new wave of employees with diverse needs, demands and values. New technologies offer many opportunities and possibilities in the reduction of decision-making bias, particularly within the many work structures, systems and practices that have so often been the cause of workplace prejudice.

References

Acker, J. (1990). Hierarchies, jobs, bodies: A theory of gendered organizations. *Gender and Society, 4*(2), 139–158. https://doi.org/10.1177/089124390004002002

Acker, J. (2006). Inequality regimes: Gender, class, and race in organizations. *Gender and Society, 20*(4), 441–464. https://doi.org/10.1177/0891243206289499

Allport, G. W. (1954). *The nature of prejudice*. Addison-Wesley.

Astley, M., & Cherkashyna, O. (2021). *Developing Diversity Strategies using HR Analytics*. Unpublished manuscript.

Berkowitz, L. (2000). *Causes and consequences of feelings*. Cambridge University Press. https://doi.org/10.1017/CBO9780511606106

Bosak, J., Sczesny, S., & Eagly, A. H. (2012). The impact of social roles on trait judgments: A critical reexamination. *Personality and Social Psychology Bulletin, 38*(4), 429–440. https://doi.org/10.1177/0146167211427308

Bowser, B. P. (2017). Racism: Origin and theory. *Journal of Black Studies, 48*(6), 572–590. https://doi.org/10.1177/0021934717702135

Deaux, K., & Kite, M. (1993). Gender stereotypes. In F. L. Denmark & M. A. Paludi (Eds.), *Psychology of women: A handbook of issues and theories* (pp. 107–139). Greenwood Press/Greenwood Publishing Group.

Davis, A. Y. (1983). *Women, race and class*. Black women writers series.

Denham, A. (2018). The gig economy is the future and women can lead the charge. *The Telegraph*, April 11. https://www.telegraph.co.uk/women/business/everyone-benefiting-gig-economy-apart-women/

Eagly, A. H. (1987). *Sex differences in social behaviour: A social role interpretation*. Erlbaum.

Eagly, A. H. (1997). Sex differences in social behavior: Comparing social role theory and evolutionary psychology. *American Psychologist, 52*(12), 1380–1383. https://doi.org/10.1037/0003-066X.52.12.1380.b

Eagly, A. H., & Steffen, V. J. (1984). Gender stereotypes stem from the distribution of women and men into social roles. *Journal of Personality and Social Psychology, 46*(4), 735–754. https://doi.org/10.1037/0022-3514.46.4.735

Fazio, R. H. (1986). How do attitudes guide behaviour? In R. M. Sorrentino & E. T. Higgins (Eds.), *Handbook of motivation and cognition: Foundations of social behaviour* (Vol. 1, pp. 204–243). Guilford Press.

Fazio, R. H. (1995). Attitudes as object-evaluation associations: Determinants, consequences, and correlates of attitude accessibility. In R. E. Petty & J. A. Krosnick (Eds.), *Attitude strength: Antecedents and consequences* (pp. 247–282). Erlbaum.

George, J. (2021). A lesson on critical race theory. https://www.americanbar.org/groups/crsj/publications/human_rights_magazine_home/civil-rights-reimagining-policing/a-lesson-on-critical-race-theory/

Howcroft, D., & Rubery, J. (2019). 'Bias in, Bias out': Gender equality and the future of work debate. *Labour and Industry: A Journal of the Social and Economic Relations of Work, 29*(2), 213–227. https://doi.org/10.1080/10301763.2019.1619986

Jivani, A. I. (2020). Gender lens to the future of work. *Daedalus, 149*(1), 134–143. https://doi.org/10.1162/daed_a_01778

Kaiser-Schatzlein, R. (2022, March 15). *How Life as a Trucker Devolved Into a Dystopian Nightmare*. The New York Times.

Kelliher, C., & Anderson, D. (2010). Doing more with less? Flexible working practices and the intensification of work. *Human Relations, 63*(1), 83–106. https://doi.org/10.1177/0018726709349199

Kossek, E. E., & Lautsch, B. A. (2012). Work–family boundary management styles in organizations: A cross-level model. *Organizational Psychology Review, 2*(2), 152–171. https://doi.org/10.1177/2041386611436264

Krech, D., Crutchfield, R. S., & Ballachey, E. L. (1962). *Individual in society: A textbook of social psychology*. McGraw-Hill.

McKinsey Global Institute. (2019). The future of women at work: Transitions in the age of automation. Retrieved November 22, 2021, from https://www.mckinsey.com/featured-insights/gender-equality/the-future-of-women-at-work-transitions-in-the-age-of-automation

Nelson, T. D. (2004). *Ageism: Stereotyping and prejudice against older persons*. MIT Press.

OECD, Policy Brief. (2017). Going Digital: The Future of Work for Women. *Policy Brief on the Future of Work*.

OECD. (2021). *Teleworking in the COVID-19 pandemic: Trends and prospects*. OECD. https://www.oecd.org/coronavirus/policy-responses/teleworking-in-the-covid-19-pandemic-trends-and-prospects-72a416b6/

Ozkazanc-Pan, B. (2021). Diversity and future of work: Inequality abound or opportunities for all?. *Management Decision, 59*(11), 2645–2659. https://doi.org/10.1108/MD-02-2019-0244

Parry, E., & McCarthy, J. (2017). *The Palgrave handbook of age diversity and work*. Retrieved March 5, 2022, from https://link.springer.com/content/pdf/10.1057/978-1-137-46781-2.pdf

Ray, V. (2019). A theory of racialized organizations. *American Sociological Review, 84*(1), 26–53. https://doi.org/10.1177/0003122418822335

Rubery, J., Grimshaw, D., Hebson, G., & Ugarte, S. (2015). "It's all about time": Time as contested terrain in the management and experience of domiciliary care work in England. *Human Resource Management, 54*, 753–772.

Stevenson, B. (2021). Women, work, and families: Recovering from the pandemic-induced recession, 16.

Wajcman, J. (2018). Digital technology, work extension and the acceleration society. *German Journal of Human Resource Management, 32*(3–4), 168–176. https://doi.org/10.1177/2397002218775930

Whitehouse, G., & Brady, M. (2019). Editorial: New social inequalities and the future of work. *Labour and Industry: A Journal of the Social and Economic Relations of Work, 29*(3), 238–242. https://doi.org/10.1080/10301763.2019.1679422

CHAPTER 8

Higher Education and Skills for the Future(s) of Work

Shirley Davey and Brian Harney

Abstract This chapter takes a macro-level approach to explore key skills required for the future(s) of work in a digital era. It will explore how the future skills highlighted both impact on, and can be co-created and nurtured through, formal yet flexible higher education. Our focus is purposefully on skills for the future (not of the future) and on futures (plural). A key underpinning to our argument is the need for a narrative that moves away from a technical focus on skill development to a more holistic view of human-centred development. This is discussed with respect to the human aspects of digitalisation in virtual and real dimensions, the slow movement and elevated well-being. In providing an infrastructure which balances reflection and action while locating digital disruption in its socio-economic context, higher education can ultimately provide a platform for greater certainty and progress in an age of digital disruption and uncertainty.

S. Davey (✉)
Ulster University Business School, Ulster University, Belfast, UK
e-mail: s.davey@ulster.ac.uk

B. Harney
DCU Business School, Dublin City University, Dublin, Ireland
e-mail: brian.harney@dcu.ie

T. Lynn et al. (eds.), *The Future of Work*, Palgrave Studies in Digital Business & Enabling Technologies,
https://doi.org/10.1007/978-3-031-31494-0_8

Keywords Higher education, Future of Work • Skills • Slow movement • Education • Well-being

8.1 Rationale and Motivation

Higher education institutions always face the challenge of being both timeless and timely. The evolution of on-line learning platforms, micro-credentials, virtual reality and corporate universities provides a stark reminder that the university infrastructure and modus operandi is "as old as those Manchester mills, based on a calendar that dates from a time when students had to go home to help with the harvest" (Marcus, 2020). Increased change brought about by developments in Artificial Intelligence (AI), robotics and digitalisation highlights the requirement for universities to (re)consider the role, impact and relevance of higher education in effectively contributing to a new era of work (Krishnan, 2020). This includes the challenge of changing career expectations and anchors with surveys highlighting that future students are likely to opt for becoming YouTubers or Vloggers over more traditional vocations like becoming a doctor or a fireperson (Berger, 2019). Universities are uniquely positioned to prepare students as future practitioners for emerging digital landscapes, including the ethical dilemmas and key strategic challenges that they will confront as citizens in the digital society. Equally, universities can sensitise students to the multiple possibilities for digital disruption to enhance the quality and experience of jobs, working lives, and venture creation.

This chapter explores the role of higher education institutions in fostering the education and skills required for the Future of Work. Higher education is built on a linear model founded on gradual certification of knowledge and skills, playing a formative role in the development of students, while equally serving the demands of labour markets. Digital disruption offers distinct challenges and opportunities in each of these domains. In the first section of this chapter, we detail growing demand and pressure coming from the evolution of work, mapping out key implications for the skills developed through higher education. Here we see a focus on skills for the Future of Work, with much of the impetus coming from economic bodies and policy think-tanks, as well as private sector consultancy houses. This discourse and dominant understanding narrowly frame the role and impact of universities. By contrast, the second section offers an alternative viewpoint providing a more holistic anchor to the long-term merits and imprints of university experience which recognises the multiple realities and futures of work.

8.2 Higher Education and Skills for the Future of Work: Current Emphasis

Headline statistics on the Future of Work highlight a landscape characterised by change and challenge. According to the Institute of the Future, 85% of the jobs that today's students will do in 2030 do not yet exist. Rapidly growing technologies including mobile computing and cloud computing, coupled with the Internet of Things and the rise of the metaverse, mean that the availability of appropriate skills and upskilling in the face of automation is a pressing concern for CEOs. It is therefore unsurprising that some refer to the need for "future fit" employees, mandating a "pipeline from the classroom to the workplace so the skills taught today match the skills that'll be in demand tomorrow" (Caplan, 2018). Questioning the relevance of the education system, Krishnan (2020) stresses the need to "update education with job readiness", stressing the ability "to compete against smart machines" with the "creation of long-term economic value in mind". Underpinning a discourse of upskilling and reskilling mandated by a, if not the, Future of Work is a number of high-level policy documents. For example, in its Future of Jobs Report, the World Economic Forum called out the growing significance of skills such as analytical thinking and innovation, critical thinking, complex problem solving and the use of technology (World Economic Forum, 2018).

As well as enhancing technical skills, consulting houses firms emphasise the need to focus on human capabilities such as relationship building, teamwork and leadership, as well as entrepreneurship and soft skills (Deloitte, 2019; PwC, 2019). Interestingly absent from many considerations are broader concerns related to the purpose and community of organisations manifest as stakeholder management or values related to sustainability and ethics. Following this logic, it is easy to glorify the leadership principles of mammoth organisations such as Amazon or Facebook, without inviting any consideration of their impact on working conditions and experiences of work or indeed on society more broadly (Harney & Dundon, 2020). In this vein, pedagogy often remains rooted in a functional, transmission-focused mind-set so that even when students do engage in problem-solving approaches, there is a preoccupation with reaching a fixed solution whereby students "make assumptions [rather] than examine them" (Bridgman et al., 2018, p. 447). It is perhaps unsurprising to see a convergence of desired graduate skills or attributes emphasising critical thinking, global awareness and digital literacy underscored by the need to foster "employability" (Allen et al., 2019).

Students equally have changing expectations and requirements as so-called new learners, including the means by which they access, evaluate and disseminate knowledge (Thompson, 2013). According to some critiques, an era of "ubiquitous disruption and unpredictable job evolution" means that the provision of knowledge associated with a university degree is open to question (Chamorro-Premuzic & Frankiewicz, 2019). For some, the solutions reside in more bite-size educational provisions in the form of micro-credentials, lifelong learning and accelerated industry education (Horton, 2020). Research evidence suggests otherwise, at least on some fronts. A survey of 18,000 employees across 15 countries found that those who had obtained a higher education degree had higher than average proficiency scores across cognitive, digital, interpersonal and self-leadership skill categories. Delving deeper, however, reveals some worrying insights as those elements with the weakest correlation to education included the likes of digital ethics, coping with uncertainty, empathy, creativity and imagination, courage and risk taking, coaching and synthesising messages (Dondi et al., 2021). Surveys of students find that less than half feel that their education experience has sufficiently prepared them for their chosen career (Pearson Education Report, 2020). However, the same survey notes that education was seen as an important career steppingstone playing an important role in personal development and informing "personal identity".

At the heart of the debate is whether the role of university is to provide narrow skills targeted at employability or to provide students with an infrastructure enabling them to flourish in all their endeavours. Arguably, some of the discourse and dominant understanding, fanned by private sector-led consultancy reports and economic logic, have narrowly framed the role and impact of universities. By contrast, the following section offers an alternative viewpoint which provides a more holistic anchor to the long-term merits and imprints of university experience, beyond the immediacy of skills on demand or reaching specific employment requirements. As recently articulated by Grant (2021) in his treatise "Think Again", the role of higher education in society is to stoke curiosity, fuel discovery, foster debate, encourage critical thinking and develop the next generation into more sophisticated learners.

8.3 Higher Education and Skills of the Futures of Work: An Alternative Framing

For as long as the Future of Work discourse has had currency, there have been those that have cautioned against grand narratives and futurology associated with simplistic or overly deterministic portrayals (Nolan & Wood, 2003). Predictions and concerns about the automation of education and work and the displacement of jobs and learning echo through generations (e.g., Noble, 1998). While the Covid-19 pandemic has dramatically evidenced the impact of digital disruption, it has equally highlighted key fault lines with respect to access, gender, ethnicity and class (Spicer, 2020). Digital divides exist based on uneven access, use and outcomes of digital technologies, while deficits in digital literacy can result in the exclusion of many citizens from a digital society (Lythreatis et al., 2021). Mainstream Future of Work discourse tends to gloss over broader material inequalities, assuming access, infrastructure and opportunity as a given. Less evidenced in discussions are concerns about increasing inequality, coupled with deterioration in job quality and security of employment (Ainsworth & Knox, 2021; Colfer et al., 2023). This equally holds true for those working in higher education, where it has been argued that digitalisation has fostered standardisation and degradation of working conditions while simultaneously blurring work/life boundaries (Ivancheva & Garvey, 2022). This aligns with criticism of the neo-liberal agenda and associated short-termism which risks infiltrating and colonising both the purpose and processes of higher education. Michael D. Higgins, President of Ireland, has forewarned that:

> *We must confront a prevalent, flawed and dangerous perception that the necessary focus of higher education must be on that which is exclusively utilitarian in a narrow sense, immediately applicable, and whose value is seen solely in financial or economic terms. Such a view sees the primary purpose of the university, and those who study within it, as being in preparation for a specific role within the labour market, often at the cost of the development of wider life enhancing skills, including creativity, analytical thinking. These are the skills that will be essential to the citizens of the future to make informed choices about life/work balance, about what constitutes survival and consumption, and what is meant by human flourishing, solidarity or humanity itself.* (Higgins, 2016)

From this reading there is a risk that the Future of Work discourse, informed and fuelled as it is by private sector concerns, serves as the ultimate Trojan horse in bringing neo-liberal ideals to bear to inform and determine the purpose and outcomes of higher education. While relational dimensions are incorporated into the Future of Work, for example collaboration, inclusiveness and conflict (Dondi et al., 2021), a functional agenda means that these are associated with delivering a particular, predetermined end.

Zuboff (2019) cautions against "prediction products" founded on the unprecedented methodological prowess and behavioural data collected by big business as enabled through technology. The inherent risk is that academia becomes displaced by corporate research driven by profit maximisation seeking "not only to predict our behavioural futures but also intervene in them", meaning universities could easily find themselves subject to "profitable but dystopian future developments" (Gümüsay & Reinecke, 2021). The dangers of immediacy and commercial goals in a higher education setting are long recognised serving to reinforce "just how selective we are about the topics we deem it possible to educate ourselves in" (De Botton, 2019, p. 1). Moreover, there is an inherent risk that even if higher education institutions attempt to exclusively address corporate employment demands, face-paced companies become impatient and ultimately circumvent higher education in order to meet their own rapidly shifting competitive needs (Brown, 2020; Horn, 2020).

An alternative framing requires a (re)claiming of personal agency for students so that higher education provides an infrastructure whereby they learn to engage, explore and critique. Some higher education institutions have made progress in this regard, focusing on graduate attributes that go beyond discipline specific and technical skills, including "qualities that also prepare graduates as agents of social good in an unknown future" (Barrie, 2007, p. 440). In this sense the redundancy of predicting the future is recognised and students are enabled to "be ready for many different possible futures that could unfold" (Rinne, 2021), including a privileging of their role in co-creating and creatively articulating desirable futures. This approach goes some way to confronting the challenges of technological determinism, on the one hand, and inadvertently perpetuating a neo-liberal agenda, on the other hand.

It is beyond the remit of this chapter to provide any comprehensive overview of possibilities; instead, our focus is to point to three areas particularly appropriate to the gestation of this alternative knowledge providing platforms to prompt greater agency and agile understanding (Jackson, 2019). These are purposefully provocative, in that while they could be read as agnostic to technological change, arguably they take on greater salience in the context of such change.

8.3.1 Slow Thinking

Rather than focus exclusively on speed and disruption, there is a need to rebalance educational provisions to privilege greater thought and philosophy. It is clear that the pace of digital technology development has outstripped the pace of reflection with the consequence that “deep thinking is often the illustrious casualty in the digital revolution” (Forni, 2011, p. 3). Useful inspiration can be found in the slow movement born of criticism of fast food and now part of movements across the globe, for example slow city, slow living, slow travel (Honore, 2004) and even slow professor (Berg & Seeber, 2016). Slow movements are useful to consider on a number of fronts. First, they provide a counter to the prioritisation of speed and efficiency. The focus is not on the rate at which knowledge is produced or solutions reached, but rather the quality of such outcomes (Ulmer, 2017). Second, slow movements are founded upon the concepts of self-awareness and purposeful learning, highlighting the value of immersing oneself in the current moment as opposed to chasing the next shiny bright thing. Third, it follows from this understanding that dedication, focus, failure, deep learning and a long-term emphasis are all virtues to be praised and encouraged versus deficiencies to be addressed. Fourth, the slow movement serves as a means to directly confront the “always on activity bias” associated with the rise and diffusion of digital technologies (Staats, 2019).

Slow is not simply a way of thinking but a mode of being, something of a global awakening on the quality of life inherently related to the broader social justice and environmental movements. Importantly, slow does not mean unproductive but rather “differently productive” (Ulmer, 2017). Engaging with the apparatus of the slow movement provides one way to equip students “to face uncertainties and address problems not susceptible to inquiry based on pure analytical skills” (Sarooghi et al., 2019, p. 78). The focus therefore becomes one of generative or exploratory learning, providing a life-skill in the assessment and evaluation of evidence which re-centres the ability to learn, as genuine curiosity paired with openness (Newman & Wallace, 2020). Ironically, such a foundation might provide for a more tenable and strategic contribution enabling wider and deeper connections across eco-systems and providing sensitivity and awareness to contextual trends and insights just as important as fast-moving technologies (Reeves & Whitaker, 2018; Satell, 2019).

8.3.2 Elevating Well-being

Much of the Future of Work literature risks treating individuals as "objects" as opposed to "subjects" whose dignity and worth exists independent of an organisation or job (Wright, 2020). This highlights the value of exposing students, as future employees, to the tensions and paradoxes inherent to capitalist workplaces. As per Yuval Noah Harari in thinking about future implications, including the impact of AI "Karl Marx is still a better guide then Steven Spielberg" (Harari, 2018, p. 246). Employment dynamics, and how they are addressed by organisations, will likely inform the choices students make about their future work and contribution to society. It is perhaps unsurprising that the OECD (2020) has recently called for a "redefining" of the growth narrative "to put the well-being of people at the centre of our efforts". New Zealand is exemplary here in moving away from narrow gross domestic product measures of economic success to focus on happiness and well-being as key indicators of progress (Ellsmoor, 2021). Educators can use new referents as cases and examples, drawing on cooperatives, urban gardens and social enterprises which prioritise ecological sustainability and well-being (Banerjee & Arjaliès, 2021). It will be increasingly important for students to be able to reflect and articulate what makes for sufficient growth and the necessity for frugal and conscious innovation. Insights about well-being also crossover to the role and impact of technology with students of today born into a technology-first society with little critical analysis of the extent of technology use and engagement which has become normalised. Encouragingly, there is evidence that more holistic graduate outcomes are being considered at policy level with "graduate voice" and attributes of "eudemonic" well-being such as the meaningfulness or importance of activity to graduates being incorporated into destination of leavers in higher education surveys (CABS, 2022). This leads to important considerations around health literacy and the human costs of technological performance and the pre-dominance of positive thinking and growth mind-sets, at the expense of just being, not knowing and failing (Pfeffer, 2016). With this focus students are encouraged to explore whether technological change is likely to result in greater equality or simply reproduce or reinforce existing patterns of educational, economic and social inequalities (Brown, 2020).

8.3.3 *Human Transformation in the Virtual Era*

We are human beings, never human doings. The balancing act between human and non-human actors in sharing knowledge in any organisation creates an emerging paradigm (Harney & Collings, 2021). Digital is so deeply embedded in our lives that we often overlook the magnitude of its transformative effect. There is a rising demand for tech-innovation, cyber-physical systems, alongside data acquisition and analytics to support decision making. Co-bots, originally defined as novel technological manufacturing systems, are today able to work with a certain degree of dexterity and in conjunction with humans in the same physical workspace (Bauer et al., 2016) in many industries. With AI, manifested by machines that exhibit aspects of human intelligence (HI), being increasingly utilised in many sectors, there is a need to create a symbiotic relationship between humans and machines (Huang & Rust, 2018). The power of AI in collaborative decision making is already widely recognised; indeed, Deep Knowledge Ventures, which focuses on drugs for age-related diseases, has appointed an AI algorithm, called Vital, to its board of directors (BBC, 2014).

An organisation's response to digital disruption should focus on people and processes (Kane et al., 2019). We now live in a world where any company can tap into the talent cloud to identify the highest-quality, lowest cost actor, be that technological or human for a particular task (McGowan, 2020). In this reality, we must focus on how humans uniquely add value, leveraging, not competing with, rising technology. Professionals in the near future must learn to not only utilise but collaborate with AI, avatars and co-bots in both the real and virtual worlds. What education should do to support this is to empower learners to unlock their potential in these virtual dimensions and aspects of collaboration, in order to:

- be secure, education should be the anchor nurturing FoW skills;
- break new ground, vanquishing new worlds be they virtual or real, and proceeding away from the status quo towards learning for life;

- build beyond boundaries, education like business is a contact sport and transdisciplinary learning is key. Students should be prepared to journey in different disciplines.

The beauty of the current situation is that because we have built highly sophisticated AI that can learn, we have also built AI that can help us develop far more sophisticated and secure human intelligence (OECD, 2018). An intelligent approach to AI in education, including working with AI developers, is essential to address and co-create the best of AI and HI.

In recent years, the metaverse has attracted enormous attention from around the world with the development of related technologies (Duan et al., 2021). As technology advances and consumes more routine work, the value of work requiring organic cognition increases. Research from Australia on "Peak Human potential" (Gallagher, 2019) found that the more an industry is disrupted by digital technologies, the more that workers value uniquely human "social competencies". To maximise human potential, we need to put humans at the centre of every value creation process, augmenting human capacity with ever more capable tools. Today's talent must embrace change and importantly, they must be able to navigate it.

8.4 Conclusion

Higher education institutions provide a critical infrastructure for "practitioners in training" to develop skills in order to effectively explore, navigate and co-create the future(s) for work. This chapter has focused on a move away from instrumental and utilitarian education towards embracing a more holistic approach which at once privileges asking and answering questions. While recognising immediate demands from employers for input into the analysis and design of education, they should form the beginning rather than the end of such assessment. Too often considerations focus on the "bright shiny" new object, to the neglect of what remains the same.

A key part of our argument is that more attention needs to be directed to the agents tasked with creating the futures of work, both students and educators. A consideration of the slow movement prompts a re-insertion of the human and humane in attuning awareness and providing students with the tools and infrastructure to be qualitative researchers of their own experiences (Markham, 2019; Tett, 2021). It is also important to note that students' enthusiastic appreciation and interest cannot be presupposed, while formative choices and learnings are made prior to reaching higher education (Allen & Simpson, 2019; OECD, 2019). Educators also need to reflect, refresh and assess the impact of their own engagement with digital technologies to "open up the walls of the classroom in new directions" (Adler, 2015, p. 189). There are a range of higher education stakeholders with an ability to influence the student experience.

In the effort to be both timeless and timely, universities risk either being complicit in reproducing the ills of the current system or serving as harbingers of change and enhanced understanding. The role of higher education is not to prepare students for a given Future of Work based on fixed disciplinary knowledge and a predetermined career trajectory. Instead, education should prepare students for the various futures of work, providing them with innate capabilities and strategic awareness grounded on an ability to ask the right questions, to critically analyse, to explore silences and inequities, and to seek their own wisdom. This infrastructure of skills will provide a basis for wisdom and insight necessary to strive in an age of digital disruption and mass uncertainty.

References

Adler, P. (2015). 2015 Presidential Address: Our teaching mission. *Academy of Management Review, 41*(2), 185–195.

Ainsworth, S., & Knox, A. (2021). "A bridge too far?" Ideas, employment relations and policy-making about the future of work. *Industrial Relations: A Journal of Economy and Society.*

Allen, D., & Simpson, C. (2019). Inquiry into graduate attributes: Reviewing the formal and informal management curricula. *Journal of Management Education, 43*(4), 330–358.

Allen, S., Cunliffe, A. L., & Easterby-Smith, M. (2019). Understanding sustainability through the lens of ecocentric radical-reflexivity: Implications for management education. *Journal of Business Ethics, 154*(3), 781–795.

Banerjee, S. B., & Arjaliès, D.-L. (2021). Celebrating the end of enlightenment: Organization theory in the age of the Anthropocene and Gaia (and why neither is the solution to our ecological crisis). *Organization Theory, 2*(4).

Barrie, S. C. (2007). A conceptual framework for the teaching and learning of generic graduate attributes. *Studies in Higher Education, 32*, 439–458.

Bauer, W., Bender, M., Braun, M., Rally, P., & Scholtz, O. (2016). *Lightweight robots in manual assembly, best to start simply. Examining companies' initial experiences with lightweight robots*. Stuttgart.

BBC. (2014). 'Algorithm appointed board director'. BBC Technology News, 16 May 2014. Retrieved December 2021, from https://www.bbc.co.uk/news/technology-27426942

Berg, M., & Seeber, B. (2016). *The slow professor: Challenging the culture of speed in the academy*. University of Toronto Press.

Berger, E. (2019). American kids would much rather be YouTubers than astronauts.https://arstechnica.com/science/2019/07/american-kids-would-much-rather-be-youtubers-than-astronauts/

Bridgman, T., McLaughlin, C., & Cummings, S. (2018). Overcoming the problem with solving business problems: Using theory differently to rejuvenate the case method for turbulent times. *Journal of Management Education, 42*(4), 441–460.

Brown, P. (2020). Some observations on the race to higher education, digital technologies and the future of work. *Journal of Education and Work, 33*(7–8), 491–499.

CABS. (2022). Graduate outcomes in 'Business & Administrative Studies': Analysis of the second year of results from the new HESA survey. Retrieved December 2021, from https://charteredabs.org/graduate-outcomes-in-business-administrative-studies-analysis-of-the-second-year-of-results-from-the-new-hesa-survey/

Caplan, S. (2018). Closing the skills gap could be as simple as ABC. *Strategy & Business*, 19 November.

Chamorro-Premuzic, T., & Frankiewicz, B. (2019). Does higher education still prepare people for jobs? *Harvard Business Review*. https://hbr.org/2019/01/does-higher-education-still-prepare-people-for-jobs

Colfer, B., Harney, B., McLaughlin, C., & Wright, C. (Eds.). (2023). *Protecting the future of work: New institutional arrangements for safeguarding labour standards*. Bingley.

De Botton, A. (2019). *Introduction: The school of life: An emotional education*. Hamish Hamilton.

Deloitte. (2019). *Leading the social enterprise: Reinvent with a human focus*. Deloitte Human Capital Trends.

Dondi, M., Klier, J., Panier, F., & Jörg, S. (2021). Defining the skills citizens will need in the future world of work. *McKinsey Insight*.

Duan, H., Li, J., Fan, S., Lin, Z., Wu, X., & Cai, W. (2021, October). Metaverse for social good: A university campus prototype. In *Proceedings of the 29th ACM International Conference on Multimedia* (pp. 153–161). ACM Digital Library.

Ellsmoor, J. (2021). New Zealand ditches GDP for happiness and wellbeing. https://www.forbes.com/sites/jamesellsmoor/2019/07/11/new-zealand-ditches-gdp-for-happiness-and-wellbeing/

Forni, P. M. (2011). *The thinking life: How to thrive in the age of distraction*. St Martin's Press.

Gallagher, P. (2019). Peak human potential: Preparing workers for the digital economy. Retrieved December 2021, from https://www.swinburne.edu.au/news/2019/06/peak-human-potential-preparing-workers-for-the-digital-economy/

Grant, A. (2021). *Think again*. WH Allen.

Gümüsay, A. A., & Reinecke, J. (2021). Researching for desirable futures: From real Utopias to imagining alternatives. *Journal of Management Studies*.

Harari, Y. N. (2018). *21 lessons for the 21st century*. Jonathan Cape.

Harney, B., & Collings, D. G. (2021). Navigating the shifting landscapes of HRM. *Human Resource Management Review, 31*(4), 1–9.

Harney, B., & Dundon, T. (2020). Amazon: HRM and change in the house of neo-liberalism. In T. Dundon & A. Wilkinson (Eds.), *Case studies in work, Employment and human resource management* (pp. 191–199). Elgar.

Higgins, M. D. (2016) Speech at the EUA Annual Conference, NUI Galway 7th of April. https://www.president.ie/en/media-library/speeches/speech-by-president-michael-d-higgins-eua-annual-conference

Honore, C. (2004). *In praise of slow: How a worldwide movement is challenging the cult of speed*. Orion.

Horn, B. (2020). Education, disrupted. *MIT Sloan Management Review*.

Horton, A. P. (2020). Could micro-credentials compete with traditional degrees? Retrieved December 2021, from https://www.bbc.com/worklife/article/20200212-could-micro-credentials-compete-with-traditional-degrees

Huang, M. H., & Rust, R. T. (2018). Artificial intelligence in service. *Journal of Service Research, 21*(2), 155–172.

Ivancheva, M., & Garvey, B. (2022). Putting the university to work: The subsumption of academic labour in UK's shift to digital higher education. *New Technology, Work and Employment*. https://doi.org/10.1111/ntwe.12237

Jackson, N. C. (2019). Managing for competency with innovation change in higher education: Examining the pitfalls and pivots of digital transformation. *Business Horizons, 62*(6), 761–772.

Kane, G. C., Phillips, A. N., Copulsky, J., & Andrus, G. (2019). How digital leadership is (n't) different. *MIT Sloan Management Review, 60*(3), 34–39.

Krishnan, N. (2020). Our education system is losing relevance. Here's how to unleash its potential, World Economic Forum. 13th of April 2020. Available at https://www.weforum.org/agenda/2020/04/our-education-system-is-losingrelevance-heres-how-to-update-it/. Accessed 10th of May 2023.

Lythreatis, S., Singh, S. K., & El-Kassar, A.-N. (2021). The digital divide: A review and future research agenda. *Technological Forecasting and Social Change*.

Marcus, J. (2020). How technology is changing the future of higher education. *New York Times*.

Markham, A. N. (2019). Critical pedagogy as a response to datafication. *Qualitative Inquiry, 25*(8), 754–760.
McGowan, H. E., & Shipley, C. (2020). *The adaptation advantage: Let go, learn fast, and thrive in the future of work.* John Wiley & Sons.
Newman, S., & Wallace, W. (2020). *Thinking productively about the future. Strategy & Business.*
Noble, D. F. (1998). Digital diploma mills: The automation of higher education. *Science as Culture, 7*(3), 355–368.
Nolan, P., & Wood, S. (2003). Mapping the future of work. *British Journal of Industrial Relations, 41*(2), 165–174.
OECD. (2018). Preparing humanity for change and artificial intelligence: Future of Education and Skills 2030: Curriculum Analysis. OECD Publishing. Retrieved November 2021, from: https://www.oecd.org/education/2030/Preparing-humanity-for-change-and-artificial-intelligence.pdf
OECD. (2019). *Education at a glance 2019: OECD indicators.* OECD Publishing.
OECD. (2020). *Beyond growth: Towards a new economic approach.* OECD Publishing.
Pearson. (2020). Global Learners Survey. August 2020 Available at https://plc.pearson.com/sites/pearson-corp/files/footer-image/pearson-global-learners-survey-2020.pdf (last accessed 10th of May, 2023).
Pfeffer, J. (2016). Why the assholes are winning: Money trumps all. *Journal of Management Studies, 53*(4), 663–669.
PwC. (2019). *Talent trends 2019.* PwC.
Reeves, M., & Whitaker, K. (2018). *Competing on the rate of learning.* Boston Consulting Group.
Rinne, A. (2021). A Futurist's guide to preparing your company for constant change. *Harvard Business Review.* https://hbr.org/2021/09/a-futurists-guide-to-preparing-your-company-for-constant-change
Sarooghi, H., Sunny, S., Hornsby, J., & Fernhaber, S. (2019). Design thinking and entrepreneurship education: Where are we, and what are the possibilities? *Journal of Small Business Management, 57*, 78–93.
Satell, G. (2019). Why "Move Fast and Break Things" doesn't work anymore. *Harvard Business Blog.*
Spicer, A. (2020). Organizational culture and COVID-19. *Journal of Management Studies.*
Staats, B. (2019). *Never stop learning: Stay relevant, re-invent yourself and thrive.* Harvard Business Review Press.
Tett, G. (2021). *Anthro-vision.* Penguin Books.
Thompson, P. (2013). The digital natives as learners: Technology use patterns and approaches to learning. *Computers & Education, 65*, 12–33.
Ulmer, J. (2017). Writing slow ontology. *Qualitative Inquiry, 23*, 201–211.

World Economic Forum. (2018). *Future of jobs report 2018*. Centre for the New Economy and Society.
Wright, P. (2020). Rediscovering the "Human" in strategic human capital. *Human Resource Management Review*. https://doi.org/10.1016/j.hrmr.2020.100781
Zuboff, S. (2019). *The age of surveillance capitalism*. Profile Book.

CHAPTER 9

Digital Learning: A Bright New Dawn for Learning and Development

Claire Gubbins, Thomas N. Garavan, and Elisabeth E. Bennett

Abstract There has been a steady increase in the use of digital learning media, a trajectory which was accelerated in recent years due to a myriad of factors. Definitions of digital learning are quite diverse but generally can be categorised into formal, informal and blended. Empirically and practically, the emphasis has been on formal digital learning. In this chapter we focus on the drivers, opportunities and challenges associated with digital learning as an approach to achieving organisational learning and development goals. Specifically, we discuss the drive for shorter, faster and cheaper

C. Gubbins (✉)
DCU Business School, Dublin City University, Dublin, Ireland
e-mail: claire.gubbins@dcu.ie

T. N. Garavan
Cork University Business School, University College Cork, Cork, Ireland
e-mail: tgaravan@ucc.ie

E. E. Bennett
Concordia University Ann Arbor, Ann Arbor, MI, USA
e-mail: Elisabeth.bennett@cuaa.edu

T. Lynn et al. (eds.), *The Future of Work*, Palgrave Studies in Digital Business & Enabling Technologies,
https://doi.org/10.1007/978-3-031-31494-0_9

training and learning methods and consider the impact on learning quality. We discuss digital learning in the context of learning pedagogy and consider the evidence and implications if digital learning methods are not designed with learning pedagogy in mind. Finally, we acknowledge the re-ignited emphasis on informal learning or learning in the flow of work and consider if digital technologies can facilitate such learning.

Keywords Digital learning • Learning and development • Learning pedagogy

9.1 Introduction

Digital technologies have restructured many facets of organisational human resource (HR) practices, and learning and development (L&D) is no different (Nachmias & Hubschmid-Vierheilig, 2021; Anderson, 2020; Garavan et al., 2020a; Li, 2013). The impact of digitial technologies on L&D depends on how they are implemented; at one end of the spectrum having the potential to disrupt existing L&D activities and at the other end incrementally supporting and complementing tried and tested classroom-based practices (CIPD, 2021; Garavan et al., 2020a). The evidence to-date points to significant growth in digital learning. For example, pre Covid-19 data indicated a steady usage of various forms of digital learning with, for example, estimates that over 57% of organisations in 2020 (pre-pandemic) implementing some form of digital learning (CIPD, 2020) compared to 29% in 2015. Prior to the pandemic many organisations were using digital learning to deliver L&D in areas such as compliance, sales, ethics and desktop application training (Training Magazine, 2019). LinkedIn Workplace Learning Report (2020) showed budgets were continuing to shift from instructor-led training (ILT) to online learning pre-Covid with 38% of those surveyed already considering a decrease in ILT versus 58% increasing online budgets. There is no doubt that the pandemic accelerated the use of various forms of digital learning (CIPD, 2021) in what was an already occurring shift to digital and online learning (Cedefop, 2020).

Digital learning has emerged as a contemporary and future trend in organisations, the L&D practitioner literature and to some extent the growing academic literature. As a relatively new phenomenon, there are variations in the terminology used. The terms "digital" and "online"

learning are being used interchangeably (Belaya, 2018), yet there are important distinctions and overlaps between both concepts. There is limited empirical evidence concerning digital learning such as, for example, how digital learning impacts the learning experience, the extent to which digital learning transfers to the job, the effectiveness of digital learning platforms for facilitating informal learning, the overall effectiveness of digital L&D and what it all means for the future roles of L&D professionals. The purpose of this chapter is to define and conceptualise digital learning and consider some potential drivers and challenges associated with digital learning as an approach to achieving organisational L&D goals.

9.2 Conceptualising Digital Learning

The lack of a clear definition of *digital learning* is something that continues to pervade the academic and practitioner literature. For example, Anderson et al. (2016) highlighted that the term *digital* defies definition, and this results in a lack of clarity concerning the competencies required of L&D professionals and the capabilities, resources and abilities required of L&D functions. Much of the academic contributions to-date have focused on the field of Human Resource Development (HRD)—a field which studies learning and development—and the role of technology in HRD (McWhorter, 2010, 2014) under the umbrella term virtual HRD (VHRD). Bennett (2009) describes VHRD as a "rich and culturally relevant web environment that strategically improves expertise, performance, innovation and community building through formal and informal learning". Bennett (2010) also argues that VHRD does not displace the traditional focus on HRD in terms of its purposes but instead shifts the paradigm in terms of how HRD operates. VHRD incorporates career, organisation and technology development (Bennett, 2010). Thite (2022, p. 88) states that "digital HRD deals with the nature, role, and contribution of technology in strategically managing talent in a digital world. It incorporates social, mobile, analytics, cloud (SMAC) and other emerging technologies including big data, artificial intelligence (AI) and analytics for efficient and effective delivery of on-demand HRD services". This definition is all-encompassing; however, conceptualisations within L&D have a more general focus. For example, Belaya (2018) defines digital learning according to three broad and overlapping categories:

1. Formal Digital Learning: This type of digital learning uses technology to deliver formal training with limited support from or interaction with L&D professionals. It typically takes the form of narrow skills areas with clearly specified learning objectives and end-point assessments.
2. Informal Digital Learning: This type of digital learning envisages the use of technology to provide opportunities to support informal learning in organisations. It focuses on communities of practice and knowledge sharing. The emphasis here is on the role of the learner to seek out knowledge.
3. Blended or Supported Learning: This category of digital learning combines the formal and informal. It combines traditional in-person or classroom learning with online delivery options.

With respect to informal learning via digital technologies, Clark et al. (2018) add further layers. Informal learning can be (1) organised and intentional such as on-the-job training, mentoring and communities of practice or (2) everyday informal learning which is unstructured and occurs in daily work life via trial and error, learning by doing and modelling others. This further classification of informal learning results in Clark et al. (2018) identifying a continuum of informal learning opportunities which can be classified according to those that are high-touch or low-touch in terms of human interaction (high-touch) or technological interaction (low-touch). As such, when viewed through a low-touch lens, mobile technology with its ubiquitous access to information regardless of time and place has created opportunities for informal learning (Brown & Mbati, 2015).

Digital learning is also conceptualised as that which occurs through (1) synchronous engagement where learners are doing the same thing together at the same time or (2) asynchronous engagement where learners learn separately and at different times (Cleveland-Innes & Wilton, 2018). The latter envisages that learners have independence, flexibility and the ability to self-pace, whereas the former envisages a facilitator or trainer presence, immediate feedback and significant peer interaction. Other conceptualisations of digital learning highlight four distinct strands: *individual learning* whereby learners only have access to the digital learning materials provided; *trainer-assisted learning* where online learners are supported and facilitated by a trainer or instructor; *collaborative learning* which is learning that takes place via a virtual community; and *blended learning* which is conceptualised as a mixture of these different forms.

What emerges from the L&D literature is that digital learning is defined in a rather general all-encompassing way. Table 9.1 summarises a selection of digital learning technologies that come within the umbrella term of digital learning.

9.3 Digital Learning: Drivers and Challenges

There are many factors driving digital learning and transforming how learning is designed, delivered, enabled and engrained in the fabric of organisational functioning and individual's day-to-day work. Equally, for every driving factor there are challenges that require significant consideration in progressing a digital learning strategy or approach to learning within organisations. We highlight a number of these here, namely shorter, faster and cheaper training and learning methods; learning in the flow of work; and digital learning pedagogy.

9.3.1 Shorter, Faster and Cheaper Training and Learning Methods

Globalisation and technological advancement have pushed organisations to become more flexible and cost-effective when it comes to the delivery of learning (Okano et al., 2018; Thite, 2022). The ever-changing skills requirements that flow from globalisation and automation point to major shifts in the skills required of employees, thus driving the need for increased training activity. For example, the 2020 LinkedIn Workplace Learning report found that L&D professionals considered the need to close skills gaps as a key strategic priority with more than half of UK L&D professionals planning upskilling and reskilling programmes. The practitioner literature identifies that organisations and managers are demanding shortened programmes, faster novice-to-expert development time, mechanisms to train employees at scale (Scott-Jackson et al., 2015) and learning methods that are integrated into an employee's day job rather than requiring significant off-the-job attendance (Ferguson et al., 2017). These pressures, alongside a need to find cost-effective ways to deliver training, are driving the adoption of digital learning (CIPD, 2020, 2021; Cleveland-Innes & Wilton, 2018).

However, concerns still exist as to whether there is a trade-off between the quality of the learner experience and learning outcomes, on the one hand, and the need by organisations to reduce the costs and increase the

Table 9.1 Common L&D technology-based applications

Strategy	*Definition*	*Supports L&D*	*Benefits*	*Concerns*
Artificial Intelligence (AI)	Computer simulation of cognition to solve problems	Evaluation	Provides domain-specific data analysis that is either too difficult or time consuming for humans to do	It needs to be trained by humans or big data; it can have built-in flaws and biases; ethical concerns regarding the consequences for humans; general intelligence not yet achieved
Augmented Reality (AR)	The overlay of digital features to enhance the real world	Delivery	Learning more motivating when combining real elements and more senses; can include game-like design	Learner may dislike wearing VR headsets; time is needed to orient and acclimatise; may cause motion sickness; harder to do sporadically versus manual instruction
Learning Analytics	"The measurement, collection, analysis and reporting of data about learners and their contexts, for purposes of understanding and optimising learning and the environments in which it occur" (SoLAR, 2022, para. 1)	Needs analysis Evaluation Assessment Re-design	Allows for continuous improvement during and after a learning event; often uses social network analysis	Validity issues if smaller numbers of data points; continuous improvement may make statistical significance problematic; depends heavily on proper instructional design and learning objectives; data could be misinterpreted and misused

(*continued*)

Table 9.1 (continued)

Strategy	*Definition*	*Supports L&D*	*Benefits*	*Concerns*
Learning Management System (LMS)	Software system used to design, deliver and assess eLearning	Delivery Assessment Evaluation	Tools for delivery of formal courses, typically used for asynchronous learning, but offer synchronous tools; can link to external technologies and offer a wide variety of software partnerships; incorporate common features such as organised content, assignment submission, feedback, gradebooks and small groups; have been used as rudimentary intranets for VHRD in schools	Requires self-direction; expensive and cumbersome to maintain; may be overkill for smaller organisations and limited-use trainings; substantial instructor and participant learning curve; may become tedious if repetitive; software is typically hosted on another company's website or in the cloud, so confidentiality and accessibility must be addressed

(*continued*)

Table 9.1 (continued)

Strategy	*Definition*	*Supports L&D*	*Benefits*	*Concerns*
Massively Open Online Learning (MOOC)	Open access web-based course designed to allow a virtually unlimited number of participants	Delivery Assessment	Large-scale training; flexible start time; can incorporate micro-credentialing; can be curated by organisations as recommended ways to fill learning gaps	Given the volume of learners, interaction with instructors and fellow learners may be limited; assessment may be very basic and weak at assessing learning objectives; knowledge and skills may not transfer to the workplace; difficult to authenticate the learners; content may be biased for profit-making

(*continued*)

Table 9.1 (continued)

Strategy	*Definition*	*Supports L&D*	*Benefits*	*Concerns*
Online Training	Designed courses and learning encounters delivered via digital networks	Delivery Assessment Evaluation	Increasingly common, especially for onboarding and mandatory training (e.g., safety, sexual harassment, policy awareness); human designed but may or may not be instructor-led; may be linked or loaded to corporate intranets, allowing for internal or external access; can incorporate all levels of learning, including organisational culture and values	Some training activities may not translate well in online delivery; requires a different set of design and delivery skills from traditional training; relies heavily on advance design and may be difficult to adjust on-the-fly; may impede relationship-building or sense of belonging; isolated use of online training alone may not be enough for performance improvement

(*continued*)

Table 9.1 (continued)

Strategy	*Definition*	*Supports L&D*	*Benefits*	*Concerns*
Social Media	A broad term for web-based digital tools and platforms that allow members to create and share content as well as interact and learn within a networked community (Bennett, 2022)	Delivery Evaluation Re-design	Easily incorporated into L&D events and LMS through internal software or external links to commercial programmes. Support knowledge sharing, group problem-solving, reflective activities as well as community building	Potential for off-topic distractions to cost time and attention from corporate needs. Culture building could lead to us versus them identification. Comments can be misconstrued
Videoconferencing	A meeting that uses video and audio technology to facilitate interactions between two or more physical locations	Delivery	Provides a synchronous human connection across space and time; may be recorded for future review; can incorporate features, such as emotion expression through icons, hand-raising, chat, screensharing and breakout rooms; provides opportunities for information exchange, learning, building a social fabric	Social connection and knowledge sharing may be hindered if culture is unsupportive; improper meeting facilitation may reduce effectiveness; ethical concerns with how meetings are run and recorded; humans may experience fatigue being on video for an extended time

(*continued*)

Table 9.1 (continued)

Strategy	*Definition*	*Supports L&D*	*Benefits*	*Concerns*
Virtual Reality (VR)	Fully immersive digital technology that simulates the real world	Needs analysis Delivery Re-design	Allows training of high-risk skills in a relatively risk-free environment; method can be interesting and motivating; can use branching scenarios to simulate variations in responses and outcomes; allows for both linear and non-linear learning pathways; future VR may include more sophisticated haptics that improve sensory and body-based learning	Costly to produce and equip; may be overkill for basic training needs; typically requires expensive equipment; significant learning curve for trainees and may cause motion sickness; bots may seem unreal; concerns that avatar use for interactions can result in unacceptable behaviours

(*continued*)

Table 9.1 (continued)

Strategy	*Definition*	*Supports L&D*	*Benefits*	*Concerns*
Virtual Instructor-Led Training (VILT)	Training that is instructor-led in a classroom-like experience, often synchronous but may also be asynchronous (note: overlaps with online training)	Delivery Evaluation Re-design	Designed and led by human instructors that can adjust of course design, provide feedback and facilitate meaning making; instructors provide extra help or enrichment; allows for learners at multiple locations to benefit from instruction that may be housed in another geography; ensures consistency of content	Learners may get overlooked if there is a high ratio of participants to instructors; depends on strong instructional design and technology skills; may attempt to replicate traditional classroom techniques in ineffective ways; trust-building between learners and instructors may be overlooked as an important first step

(*continued*)

Table 9.1 (continued)

Strategy	*Definition*	*Supports L&D*	*Benefits*	*Concerns*
Virtual HRD	"A media-rich and culturally relevant web environment that strategically improves expertise, performance, innovation, and community-building through formal and informal learning" (Bennett, 2009, p. 364)	Design Delivery Evaluation	Views technology as an environment in which work and learning occur fluidly; recasts the role of HRD/L&D professionals and trainers as learning environment designers; emphasises the social and cultural facets to organisational technology; inclusive of but not limited to online training	HRD/L&D have been slow to adapt to the environmental view of virtual HRD; research is lagging behind practice
Webinar	A term produced by the combination of web and seminar, or a seminar delivered via internet technology	Delivery	Allows for efficient presentation of information and some discussion, often through controlled chat; can be recorded for later viewing	Often has highly specific foci; interactivity with learners difficult to achieve

(*continued*)

Table 9.1 (continued)

Strategy	*Definition*	*Supports L&D*	*Benefits*	*Concerns*
Wiki	Hypertext knowledge base managed by members whom curate and update knowledge	Delivery	Inclusive and dynamic knowledge management process that captures expertise, common terms and processes; allows anytime access to informal learning and problem-solving; searchable	Information may be stale; subject to sabotage; may reveal proprietary information; conflict may occur to determine who is able to edit; accuracy of content questioned

flexibility of delivering learning, on the other. The limited empirical evidence on the effectiveness of digital learning by comparison to traditional face-to-face learning formats points to learning disadvantages. One of the issues concerns dropout rates, which are higher than for traditional learning environments. For example, completion rates for MOOCs would appear to be particularly low (Kizilcec et al., 2020) and dropouts in asynchronous distance education substantially higher than synchronous (Bernard et al., 2004). Additional issues include: (1) the lack of familiarity of learners with digital learning platforms; (2) the inability of learners to engage in self-directed learning due to limitations in self-direction, time management and personal planning skills; (3) the lack of personal supports; (4) feelings of isolation in asynchronous digital learning contexts; (5) limited digital literacy in using hardware and software; (6) limited cognitive skills for searching, retrieving and interpreting data; (7) a need for continuous retraining to keep pace with technological developments; (8) psychological costs incurred by those required to learn in digital environments whom lack the preference or skills to do so and (9) lack of learner motivation, etc. (Montgomerie et al., 2016; Zaidi et al., 2018; Cleveland-Innes & Wilton, 2018; CIPD, 2020; Benson et al., 2002; Choudhury & Pattnaik, 2020; Ali et al., 2018).

On the other hand, further developments in the technology available for digital learning point to the potential to address some of these issues (LinkedIn Workplace Learning Report, 2020). These include: AI and machine learning to achieve more accurate personalisation of learning; virtual and augmented reality which may enable social learning and gamification; and live streams/live video and learning embedded in business applications, which could potentially enable better transfer of learning to the job.

9.3.2 *Learning Pedagogy and Digital Learning*

The digital pivot in the context of learning has major implications for how we view pedagogy (Anderson, 2020). Central to adult learning theory (Garavan et al., 2020a; James & Pollard, 2011) are such principles as (1) promoting active engagement of the learner in the learning process; (2) building on the prior experience and learning of trainees; (3) recognition of informal learning as central to the learning process and (4) promotion of continuous learning. Digital learning design requires significant consideration of how to enact these principles. However, the evidence points to a lack of acceptance of digital learning by trainers and facilitators, a lack of ownership amongst instructors of digital learning and poor technological skills (Garavan et al., 2020b; Huismann, 2020; Anderson, 2020). Educators often do not have a learning experience design approach that is supported by the recent findings of learning sciences and instructional design models with which to develop engaging, interactive and beneficial augmented reality learning experiences (Czerkawski & Berti, 2021). ILO (2020) suggested that poor preparedness of trainers and L&D professionals was particularly evident during the pandemic where L&D functions had to make very rapid shifts to digital learning platforms. CIPD (2020) highlighted that almost 50% of UK L&D professionals lack the skills to facilitate social learning online. A further difficulty is that a considerable amount of digital learning delivery is asynchronous, which minimises the potential for these principles to be embedded in the learning process.

The effective integration of many of the fundamental principles of pedagogy has to-date not received the attention that it merits in L&D and digital learning research and practice, and yet it is fundamental to designing digital learning solutions which are as effective as traditional learning approaches. It is also identified that empirical research on digitally enabled education focuses more on learning outcomes than attitudes or process skills (Antonio, 2022), and some research (e.g., on distance learning) is found to be methodologically weak and so solid conclusions can't be drawn (Bernard et al., 2004). Some meta-analyses conclude that it is not the delivery media that is most important in determining whether participants learn, but rather it is the instructional methods used (Sitzmann et al., 2006). As such if the same instructional methods are used, then web-based and classroom instruction are equally or more effective depending on the learning outcome in question (Sitzmann et al., 2006). The use of active versus passive instructional methods is found to determine whether simulation game groups or comparison groups learn more (Sitzmann & Ely, 2011). A meta-analysis on blended learning identified that the incorporation of constructivist learning strategies such as inquiry, cooperative learning, guided discovery, problem-posing strategy and game-based learning elevated the effectiveness of blended learning approaches for achieving learning outcomes. Such research illuminates how the success or failure of digital learning could be predicated on the extent to which the principles of pedagogy are considered in design.

9.3.3 *Learning in the Flow of Work*

A re-ignited view of learning is taking place with the emphasis being less about traditional training and a knowledge-push approach to learning (Gubbins & Dooley, 2021) and instead greater recognition that learning takes place in multiple settings and contexts from the formal to the informal, including from the community, family and the workplace (Natriello, 2007). Learning is a "cradle to grave" phenomenon and is diverse in terms of when, where and how it occurs. In fact, it is argued that the majority of learning in the workplace occurs through experience and informally (Tannenbaum & Cerasoli, 2013), with estimates ranging from 70% to 90% of learning taking place informally (Cerasoli et al., 2018). This reassertion of the centrality of informal learning or learning in the flow of work contrasts with approaches where learning is an "activity" divorced from work or that takes place in a classroom.

As such, perhaps the real value of digital learning technologies may reside in enabling informal digital learning. However, the sophistication of such technologies is still at exploratory stages (Anderson et al., 2016) and the empirical evidence as to its effectiveness is still very much in its infancy. Discussions around how games and simulations facilitate digitally enabled learning refer only to episodic learning. Equally or more important is the environment around these learning episodes that facilitates interaction, conversation and learning between learners via social networks (Downes, 2010). Here learning and learning needs are identified by the learner not the content provider. A preliminary piece of research comparing virtual worlds focused on gaming, social interaction or a mix identifies that structural virtual world community social capital differs significantly depending on the purpose of the virtual world (Nazir et al., 2018). As such the extent to which informal learning via social networks can occur via virtual worlds may vary according to the focus of the platform.

Virtual 3D workspaces have the potential to enable informal learning via learning from others (see Purdy, 2022) because they enable social connection and are considered more effective than 2D technologies. NextMeet, for example, includes features that permit "bump into" experiences where avatars can engage with learners in real-time for water-cooler type conversations and related informal learning. The platform has live status tracking so that just as in a physical office space, one can walk around (the virtual space) to identify who is "in" and free for a question/chat informally. Platforms, such as UneeQ, also permit connection between avatars of real-world colleagues and AI-powered human-like digital bots who can converse in natural language facilitating human-technology social interaction and learning. Informal learning behaviours which focus on observing others doing a task could be replaced with virtual reality technologies that simulate role-plays, gameplay and 3D models of technologies in the workplace which avatars can engage with. For example, Bosch and Ford developed a VR tool for electric vehicle maintenance. Medivis uses VR technology to train medical students using 3D anatomy models. The use of technology-mediated platforms for social interactions facilitates real-time online data collection which can further inform the development of both the technologies in use and the social networks of individuals and organisations. PWC's (2020) four potential future worlds emphasise how organisations and individuals need to be strategic in analysing and cultivating social networks for idea generation and execution, for innovation and for performance. There is therefore a need for sophisticated and continuous analysis of individual employee data, which could include analysis of organisational and individual social networks. Such data collection and analysis are more easily conducted in digital environments.

Despite the possibilities for informal learning inherent in the design of these platforms, the focus tends to be on the technological possibilities instead of being aligned with learning theories and informal learning principles. As previously stated, such a foundation is required in developing effective digital learning platforms and ensuring they promote and understand learning processes occurring in organisations and social contexts (Tynjälä & Häkkinen, 2005; Wang, 2011). Research on using technologies for informal workplace learning beyond Web 2.0 applications seems to be rather limited (Schumacher, 2018). Berisha-Gawlowski et al. (2021) use Tynjälä's (2013) 3-P Model of Workplace Learning to consider how digital twins, for example, could enable each of the workplace learning principles. The review concludes that there is still a lack of empirical research and challenges in technology being able to replicate in the form of digital humans or in technology being able to work with invisible but relevant learning factors. These include human autonomy, beliefs, cognitive processes, emotions, team learning, social interaction, creativity and the interrelations between these components and informal learning.

9.4 Conclusion: Is Digital Learning the Bright New Dawn for Learning and Development?

The current environment that organisations operate in has driven the adoption of digital learning and organisations are increasingly implementing digital learning solutions. However, there are many unanswered questions concerning its effectiveness. Much of the research to-date has focused on formal asynchronous digital learning and given less attention to synchronous and informal digital learning capabilities and effectiveness. Furthermore, the research to-date has focused on educational settings (Anderson et al., 2020), which limits insights into what types of workplace learning objectives can be addressed using digital learning, the extent of retention of learning and most fundamentally, the extent of transfer of learning into day-to-day job behaviour. Thus, the evidence base is not yet sufficiently robust to reach conclusions concerning the effectiveness of digital learning.

References

Ali, S., Uppal, M. A., & Gulliver, S. R. (2018). A conceptual framework highlighting e-learning implementation barriers. *Information Technology & People, 31*(1), 156–180. https://doi.org/10.1108/ITP-10-2016-0246

Anderson, L., Lanvin, B., & Van der Heyden, L. (2016). Digitalisation initiatives and corporate strategies: A few implications for talent. In B. Lanvin & P. Evans (Eds.), *The global competitiveness index 2017: Talent and technology* (pp. 51–57). INSEAD.

Anderson, V. (2020). A digital pedagogy pivot: Re-thinking higher education practice from an HRD perspective. *Human Resource Development International, 23*(4), 452–467. https://doi.org/10.1080/13678868.2020.1778999

Anderson, V., Gifford, J., & Wildman, J. (2020). An evaluation of social learning and learner outcomes in a massive open online course (MOOC): A healthcare sector case study. *Human Resource Development International, 23*(3), 208–237. https://doi.org/10.1080/13678868.2020.1721982

Antonio, R. P. (2022). Effectiveness of blended instructional approach in improving students' scientific learning outcomes: A meta- analysis. *Journal of Higher Education Theory and Practice, 22*(5), 221–239.

Belaya, V. (2018). The use of e-learning in Vocational Education and Training (VET): Systematization of existing theoretical approaches. *Journal of Education and Learning, 7*(5), 92–101.

Bennett, E. E. (2009). Virtual HRD: The intersection of knowledge management, culture and intranets. *Advances in Developing Human Resources, 11*(3), 362–374. https://doi.org/10.1177/1523422309339724

Bennett, E. E. (2010). The coming paradigm shift: Synthesis and future directions for virtual HRD. *Advances in Developing Human Resources, 12*(6), 728–741. https://doi.org/10.1177/1523422310394796

Bennett, E. E. (2022). Leveraging technology to design and deliver human resource development. In P. Holland, T. Bertram, T. Garavan, & K. Grant (Eds.), *The Emerald handbook of work, workplaces and disruptive issues in HRM* (pp. 261–276). Emerald.

Benson, A. D., Johnson, S. D., & Kuchinke, K. P. (2002). The use of technology in the digital workplace: A framework for human resource development. *Advances in Developing Human Resources, 4*(4), 393–404. https://doi.org/10.1177/15234202237518

Berisha-Gawlowski, A., Caruso, C., & Harteis, C. (2021). The concept of a digital twin and its potential for learning organisations. In D. Ifenthaler, S. Hofhues, M. Egloggstein, & C. Helbig (Eds.), *Digital transformation of learning organizations* (p. 95). Springer Open.

Bernard, R. M., Abrami, P. C., Lou, Y., Borokhovski, E., Wade, A., Wozney, L., Wallet, P. A., Fiset, M., & Huang, B. (2004). How does distance education compare with classroom instruction? A meta-analysis of the empirical literature. *Review of Educational Research, 74*(3), 379–439. https://doi.org/10.3102/00346543074003379

Brown, T. H., & Mbati, L. S. (2015). Mobile learning: Moving past the myths and embracing opportunities. *The International Review of Research in Open and Distance Learning, 16*(2), 10.19173/irrodl.v16i2.2071.

Cedefop. (2020). Digital gap during COVID-19 for VET learners at risk in Europe. *Cedefop*, June 4.

Cerasoli, C. P., Alliger, G. M., Donsbach, J. S., Mathieu, J. E., Tannenbaum, S. I., & Orvis, K. A. (2018). Antecedents and outcomes of informal learning behaviors: A meta-analysis. *Journal of Business and Psychology, 33*(2), 203–230.

Choudhury, S., & Pattnaik, S. (2020). Emerging themes in e-learning: A review from the stakeholders' perspective. *Computers & Education, 144*. https://doi.org/10.1016/j.compedu.2019.103657

CIPD. (2020). *Digital learning. Factsheet.* Chartered Institute of Personnel and Development.

CIPD. (2021). Learning and skills at work: Survey 2021. Retrieved December 6, 2021, from https://www.cipd.co.uk/Images/learning-skills-work-report-2021-1_tcm18-95433

Clark, H., Jassal, P. K., Noy, V., & Paek, P. L. (2018). A new work-and-learn framework: Forging informal and formal learning through innovative assessment design. In D. Ifenthaler (Ed.), *Digital workplace learning: Bridging formal and informal learning with digital technologies* (p. 23). Springer.

Cleveland-Innes, M., & Wilton, D. (2018). *Guide to blended learning.* Commonwealth of Learning.

Czerkawski, B., & Berti, M. (2021). Learning experience design for augmented reality. *Research in Learning Technology, 29*, 2429.

Downes, S. (2010). New technology supporting informal learning. *Journal of Emerging Technologies in Web Intelligence, 2*(1), 27–33.

Ferguson, O., Scott, S., & Towersey, G. (2017). *Learning technologies: What managers really think.* Good Practice.

Garavan, T. N., Heneghan, S., O'Brien, F., Gubbins, C., Lai, Y., Carbery, R., Duggan, J., Lannon, R., Sheehan, M., & Grant, K. (2020b). L & D Professionals in organisations: Much ambition, unfilled promise. *European Journal of Training and Development, 44*(1), 1–86. https://doi.org/10.1108/EJTD-09-2019-0166

Garavan, T. N., Hogan, C., Cahir- O'Donnell, A., & Gubbins, C. (2020a). *Learning and development in organisations: Strategy, evidence and practice.* OakTree Press.

Gubbins, C., & Dooley, L. (2021). Delineating the tacit knowledge-seeking phase of knowledge sharing: The influence of relational social capital components. *Human Resource Development Quarterly, 32*, 319–348. https://doi.org/10.1002/hrdq.21423

Huismann, A. (2020). *Vocational education and training for the future of work: Germany* (Cedefop ReferNet Thematic Perspectives Series). Cedefop.

ILO. (2020). *Summary report: E-discussion on continuing online learning and skills development in times of the COVID-19 crisis.* International Labour Organization.
James, M., & Pollard, A. (2011). TLRP's ten principles for effective pedagogy: Rationale, development, evidence, argument and impact. *Research Papers in Education, 26*(3), 275–328. https://doi.org/10.1080/02671522.2011.590007
Kizilcec, R. F., Reich, J., Yeomans, M., Dann, C., Brunskill, E., Lopez, G., Turkay, S., Williams, J. J., & Tingley, D. (2020). Scaling up behavioural science interventions in online education. *Psychological and Cognitive Sciences, 117*(26), 14900–14905. https://doi.org/10.1073/pnas.1921417117
Li, J. (2013). Web-based technology and the changing landscape of HRD. *Human Resource Development International, 16*(3), 247–250. https://doi.org/10.1080/13678868.2013.799401
LinkedIn Learning. (2020). *2020 workplace learning report: L & D in a new decade: Taking the strategic long view.* LinkedIn Learning.
McWhorter, R. R. (2010). Exploring the Emergence of Virtual Human Resource Development. *Advances in Developing Human Resources, 12*(6), 623–631. https://doi.org/10.1177/1523422310395367
McWhorter, R. R. (2014). A synthesis of new perspectives on virtual HRD. *Advances in Developing Human Resources, 16*(3), 391–401. https://doi.org/10.1177/1523422314532126
Montgomerie, K., Edwards, M., & Thorn, K. (2016). Factors influencing online learning in an organisational context. *Journal of Management Development, 35*(10), 1313–1322.
Nachmias, S., & Hubschmid-Vierheilig, E. (2021). We need to learn how to love digital learning 'again': European SMEs response to COVID-19 digital learning needs. *Human Resource Development International, 24*(2), 123–132. https://doi.org/10.1080/13678868.2021.1893503
Natriello, G. (2007). Imagining, seeking, inventing: The future of learning and the emerging discovery networks. *Learning Inquiry, 1*, 7–18. https://doi.org/10.1007/s11519-007-0005-1
Nazir, M. Hamilton, J. R., & Tee, S. (2018, December 2–6). Social capital dimensions in virtual world platforms. In *Proceedings of the 18th International Conference on Electronic Business* (pp. 578–585). ICEB.
Okano, K., Kaczmarzyk, J. R., & Gabrieli, J. D. E. (2018). Enhancing workplace digital learning by use of the science of learning. *PLoS One, 13*(10).
Purdy, M. (2022). How the metaverse could change work. *Harvard Business Review.* https://hbr.org/2022/04/how-the-metaverse-could-change-work
PWC. (2020). *Workforce of the future: The competing forces shaping 2030.* PWC.
Schumacher, C. (2018). Supporting informal workplace learning through analytics. In D. Ifenthaler (Ed.), *Digital workplace learning: Bridging formal and informal learning with digital technologies* (p. 43). Springer.

Scott-Jackson, W., Owens, S., Saldana, M., Charles, L., Green, M., Woodman, P., & Plas, L. (2015). *Learning to lead: The digital potential*. Chartered Management Institute.

Sitzmann, T., & Ely, K. (2011). A meta-analysis of self-regulated learning in work-related training and educational attainment: What we know and where we need to go. *Psychological Bulletin*, *137*, 421–442.

Sitzmann, T., Kraiger, K., Stewart, D., & Wisher, R. (2006). The comparative effectiveness of web-based and classroom instruction: A meta-analysis. *Personnel Psychology, 59*(3), 623–664.

SoLAR. (2022). *What is learning analytics?* Society for Learning Analytics Research. https://www.solaresearch.org/about/what-is-learning-analytics/

Tannenbaum, S. I., & Cerasoli, C. P. (2013). Do team and individual debriefs enhance performance? A meta-analysis. *Human Factors: The Journal of Human Factors and Ergonomics Society, 55*, 231–245.

Thite, M. (2022). Digital human resource development: Where are we? Where should we go and how do we go there? *Human Resource Development International, 25*(1), 87–103. https://doi.org/10.1080/13678868.2020.1842982

Training Magazine. (2019). 2019 Training Industry Report. *Training Magazine*, November/December.

Tynjälä, P. (2013). Toward a 3-P model of workplace learning: A literature review. *Vocations and Learning, 6*(1), 11–36. https://doi.org/10.1007/s12186-012-9091-z

Tynjälä, P., & Häkkinen, P. (2005). E-learning at work: Theoretical underpinnings and pedagogical challenges. *The Journal of Workplace Learning, 17*(5/6), 318–336.

Wang, M. (2011). Integrating organizational, social, and individual perspectives in Web 2.0-based workplace e-learning. *Information Systems Frontiers, 13*(2), 191–205.

Zaidi, A., Beadle, S., & Hannah, A. (2018). *Review of the online learning and artificial intelligence education market*. Department for Education.

CHAPTER 10

Digital Technologies and the Future of Work: An Agent-Centred Ethical Perspective Based on Goods, Norms, and Virtues

Marta Rocchi and Caleb Bernacchio

Abstract The ethical analysis related to the impact of digital technologies on the future of work needs to be conducted considering the theoretical diversity of ethics. After reviewing prominent existing approaches to ethics (utilitarianism, deontological ethics, virtue ethics), this chapter suggests the need for an agent-centred ethical perspective based on goods, norms, and virtues for the evaluation of ethical issues related to digital technologies and their impact on the future of work. Different examples illustrate the merits of this approach, helping to untangle complex issues concerning the relationship between the nature and scope of digital technologies,

M. Rocchi (✉)
DCU Business School, Irish Institute of Digital Business, Dublin City University, Dublin, Ireland
e-mail: marta.rocchi@dcu.ie

C. Bernacchio
California State University, Monterey Bay, CA, USA
e-mail: cbernacchio@csumb.edu

T. Lynn et al. (eds.), *The Future of Work*, Palgrave Studies in Digital Business & Enabling Technologies,
https://doi.org/10.1007/978-3-031-31494-0_10

regulatory needs within the new social and technological context, and the intentions and attitudes of workers towards their work, their personal flourishing, and their contribution to the good of society.

Keywords Ethics • Digital technologies • Agent-centred approach • Goods • Virtues

10.1 Introduction

The Fourth Industrial Revolution (Schwab, 2016; Schwab & Davis, 2018) generated an intense debate on the way that digital technologies should be used and on the tools of ethical analysis that are essential in defining whether or not these technologies contribute to human flourishing and to the good of society (Jasanoff, 2016; Brusoni & Vaccaro, 2017; Floridi et al., 2018; Bertolaso & Rocchi, 2022). Mobile computing, social media, big data analytics, cloud computing, and the Internet of Things can be regarded as examples of digital technologies or, more accurately, as third platform technologies (as categorised by the International Data Corporation in 2015, see also Lynn et al., 2020).

Digital technologies generate a new set of ethical questions, which will be explored in this chapter, with specific reference to the impact that digital technologies have on the future of work, especially regarding their contribution to workers' personal flourishing and to the good of society. Academic research has been slow to systematically address the question of ethics in relation to the future of work. Extensive reviews of literature in this area, such as the one presented by Balliester and Elsheikhi (2018), do not even mention the term "ethics".

A factor that contributes to the scarcity of academic research in the space of ethics and the future of work concerns the tendency to treat the ethical perspective as a stopgap, merely a way of addressing the limitations of regulatory efforts. This chapter aims to take a first step towards addressing this research gap by suggesting an agent-centred perspective which can be used to orient ethical judgement regarding the design and use of specific digital technologies in new and redesigned jobs. The agent-centred perspective considers (1) how digital technologies contribute to human flourishing and the good of society; (2) the way that norms are set so that they facilitate the realisation of these goods in this renewed social and technological context; and (3) the human traits that enable people to flourish and contribute to the good of society through their work.

The remainder of this chapter proceeds as follows. Section 10.2 presents an overview regarding the question of ethics and briefly outlines the approach to ethics that best addresses the new context of human work. Section 10.3 presents an agent-centred perspective, considering the goods, norms, and virtues necessary to evaluate the impact of digital technologies on the future of work. The final section offers some conclusions, opening avenues for further research.

10.2 What Is Ethics? Exploring Ethical Approaches and Their Capability to Analyse the Impact of Digital Technologies on the Future of Work

Ethics is commonly thought of as a way of determining right from wrong. This is not inaccurate, but it is not the whole story. Ethics like any other interesting phenomenon can only be understood within a theoretical framework. And like most other disciplines, the field of ethics is rife with theoretical diversity. While a review of all ethical theories is beyond the scope of this chapter, a broad overview of some of the major schools of thought will be helpful before considering which ethical perspective(s) would be especially useful for analysing ethical problems related to the impact of digital technologies on the future of work. The discipline of ethics is typically seen as divided between three major schools: utilitarianism, deontology, and virtue ethics (Baron et al., 1997). There is significant diversity within each of these perspectives; however, this schema is a good starting point for our purposes. There are other significant approaches to ethics, but for this article we consider these three ethical frameworks.

Utilitarianism is one form of consequentialism, the latter being a broad approach to ethics that focuses solely on promoting good outcomes (Parfit, 1984). Utilitarianism focuses on one specific type of good outcome, that is, the happiness or wellbeing of affected persons. It is also impartial in that it treats the happiness of each person as equally relevant when determining which action is right (Hooker, 2000). While this perspective contrasts with much "common sense morality" (Parfit, 1984, p. 40), in some ways it offers an intuitively plausible way of thinking about ethics. Ethics is about promoting happiness, performing actions that result in the most beneficial consequences for others.

But utilitarianism's focus on impartiality also presents significant difficulties, even on its own terms. Many of the things that most make us happy involve partiality, relationships with friends, for example, or a mother's preferential love for her child (Parfit, 1984). Likewise, intentions matter. We care about more than the benefits that flow from a friendship; we also care about the reasons why a friend acts as she does. In other words, relationships and intentions matter more than utilitarianism suggests, at least in its standard formulations (Parfit, 1984). Likewise, it is very difficult to estimate the consequences of actions and the notion of happiness may not be determinate enough to provide concrete guidance for action (MacIntyre, 2007). Because of these problems, it makes sense to look at the other ethical frameworks.

A second prominent ethical theory, commonly seen as the main counterpart of utilitarianism, is deontology, usually associated with the work of Immanuel Kant. Deontology is focused on identifying correct rules or principles, according to which actions are morally right. In the *Groundwork of the Metaphysics of Morals*, Kant (2012) famously introduced a series of principles, what he called *categorical imperatives*, which he argued are equivalent formulations of the supreme principle of morality. Perhaps the most famous of which is Kant's *Formula of Humanity*, "so act that you use humanity, in your own person as well as in the person of any other, always at the same time as an end, never merely as a means" (Kant, 2012, p. 41, italics removed). Unlike utilitarianism, the formula of humanity clearly focuses on the value of specific relationships with specific persons. It does this by refraining from aggregating ethical value, that is, not trading off harms to some for greater benefits to others. Instead, it requires people to treat others with respect, to avoid manipulating or intentionally harming others. While this principle provides some concrete guidance as to how one should act, it leaves the issue of what sort of behaviour is incompatible with humanity at an intuitive level (MacIntyre, 2007).

This problem of indeterminacy is even more evident in the *Formula of Universal Law*, "I ought never to proceed except in such a way that I could also will that my maxim should become a universal law" (Kant, 2012, p. 17). This principle is supposed to provide a test to determine whether an action is right or wrong. For example, someone considering whether it would be right to lie to get a loan with no intention of actually repaying it could apply this test. Doing so would indicate that if it became a universal practice that everyone lies whenever some benefit could be gained, then social norms concerning promising would break down. As such, a lying promise would fail this test, indicating that it would be unethical to do (see Kant, 2012). But in the case of many other actions, the outcome is not so clear. It seems possible that all sorts of horrible actions could be universal laws. Could racism, for example, be made a universal law? Plausibly, it could. The world would be a much worse place and it would be especially difficult for minorities, but it would not obviously violate Kant's test. And there may be many other actions like this, meaning that Kant's principles are unlikely to provide a sufficient way to deal with many ethical problems (Scanlon, 2011). As such, it is worth considering virtue ethics as an alternative to these two ethical theories.

Without ignoring the question of which action is right or wrong (see Hursthouse, 1999), virtue ethics focuses on a more fundamental question: What does it mean to live a flourishing life? As such, it can be considered an "agent-centred" approach (Annas, 1995), focused on living and acting well. Human flourishing involves the fulfilment of human capacities in a coherent manner throughout the course of a unified life. It considers various human capacities, emotional, intellectual, social, creative, etc., and the various social relationships, norms, values, and attitudes that are necessary to fulfil these capacities. Here, the focus of ethics is expanded to consider the role of norms and virtues in facilitating human flourishing. As such, organisational contexts, involving various forms of work, are especially important (Sison & Fontrodona, 2012). The type of work that one does and the manner in which it is performed may have a substantial impact on one's potential to live a flourishing life, especially if one's work benefits other stakeholders and enables one to develop one's capacities.

Thus, virtue ethics integrates a concern with rules and good consequences, typical of deontology and utilitarianism, into a broader analysis focused on the question of the good of the acting person (MacIntyre, 1999; Rhonheimer, 2011), asking what goods are at stake within specific social contexts and how these goods can be integrated into a unified life (MacIntyre, 2007). Considering this perspective, an analysis of digital technologies is crucial. Indeed, digital technologies are not just new tools, whose use can be analysed in the same way as we analyse the proper or improper use of other kinds of objects. Digital technologies "transform the surrounding environment and create new ontological spaces" (Russo, 2018, p. 656), constituting a new interface with reality (Capone et al., forthcoming).

From a virtue ethics perspective, we can ask a number of questions about these new technologies all linked with the issue of human flourishing. How do new technologies impact employees? Do they promote their emotional, intellectual, and professional development? How do they affect relationships at work? Do they harm employees' abilities to form meaningful relationships that contribute to flourishing lives? Likewise, how do these new technologies impact society? Do they enable more efficient and effective forms of work that benefit a range of stakeholders? Finally, what habits and virtues do these new technologies promote or inhibit? Because of its more comprehensive focus on human flourishing and the common good, virtue ethics allows for a more fine-grained analysis of new digital technologies. As such, it is an especially fruitful lens with which to consider them.

10.3 Towards an Agent-Centred Perspective for the Ethical Analysis of Digital Technologies in the Future of Work

An agent-centred ethical approach such as virtue ethics offers the necessary tools for an ethical analysis of the complex issues surrounding the impact of digital technologies on the future of work. Indeed, the introduction of digital technologies not only requires an analysis of the goodness of the outcome related to the application of a new technology to a specific profession (utilitarian approach—emphasis on the *goods*), or only an analysis of how a specific technology complies with existing norms or respect determined principles (deontological approach—emphasis on the *norms*). There is a need for a more fine-grained consideration of intertwined issues surrounding these new technologies, focused on specific *goods* that are at stake within new modes of work. We can follow Aristotle (2000) in understanding the "goods" as the objects we desire in themselves.[1] In an agent-centred ethical perspective, we can consider human flourishing (on an individual level) and the common good (on a social level) to be the ultimate goods that we seek (MacIntyre, 1999), and consider the *norms* and *virtues* that facilitate the achievement of these goods in the context of new modes of work.[2]

A brief example may help to illustrate this. In 2019, a group of Microsoft workers published a letter for the Microsoft's CEO and President, to express their criticism of the company's decision to sell the HoloLens technology to the U.S. Army for the use in combat (Lee, 2019).[3] The

[1] Aranzadi (2011) offers a simple explanation of this definition.

[2] For theoretical aspects regarding goods, norms, and virtues in an agent-centred ethical analysis, see MacIntyre (1992) and Melé (2005).

[3] For recent developments of this deal, see Browning (2021).

Microsoft workers argued that they did not want their work to be at the service of "weapons development", since they viewed their work for Microsoft as a way of empowering people and organisations.[4] Microsoft HoloLens are a mixed reality technology that works by combining different technologies (eye-tracking, hand-tracking, holographic technology, spatial mapping, and many more) in head-mounted smart glasses that enable the user to display information, create and interact with holograms, construct virtual reality settings, and much more. Applications of this technology can be found in medicine, education, manufacturing, and, in the case that drew criticism from Microsoft workers, military settings.

It may be possible to evaluate the benefits of the application of the HoloLens in military contexts and compare them to the harms they are likely to produce (as in a Utilitarian perspective) and end up with a (particularly complex) calculus of the impact of this technology in this application on overall wellbeing. But if this sort of calculation is possible (which may not be the case since accounting for all the possible benefits and harms in the long term would be extremely difficult), this sort of analysis would be likely to leave the Microsoft workers unsatisfied. Even if the benefits of military applications of HoloLens would, according to some scale, outweigh the harm, a further question remains: would these workers be justified in contributing to this harm just because it may lead to beneficial outcomes? In other words, does the mere fact of aggregate benefits absolve the Microsoft workers, leaving them without "dirty hands"? And, leaving aside responsibilities, a question of whether this kind of work is still meaningful for the workers arise too.

Only a consideration of this technology in the context of the workers' particular life narratives and characters can provide a wider perspective for the ethical consideration of this problem. Goods are not only external, tangible, and measurable components of a morally neutral conception of wellbeing as in the Utilitarian perspective; "internal goods" are also important. These are goods that are intrinsically valuable and morally salient (MacIntyre, 2007). As Moore summarises, "internal goods are of two kinds. First, there is the good product or, we may add in an organizational context, the good service. [...] Second, however, there is the internal good which involves the perfection of the practitioners engaged in the craft or practice" (Moore, 2017, p. 57). In the context of this example,

[4] The original post on Twitter can be found here: https://twitter.com/MsWorkers4/status/1099066343523930112.

the relevant internal goods include the excellence of the technology produced, which the workers view as linked directly with beneficial results for individuals and organisations, and the excellence of the life of a Microsoft worker, someone who can view herself as doing work that empowers others. This understanding of work plays an essential role in motivating these workers, and, arguably, the technologies that they have produced would have been impossible absent this morally salient conception of work at Microsoft. Thus, beyond a consideration of consequences, it is necessary to consider whether military applications of HoloLens are consistent with the ideals and virtues of the workers that have developed it, since a focus solely on outcomes is not sufficient to account for the complex system of intentions, actions, and circumstances that surround the design, development, and production of this particular digital technology. More generally, it is essential to ask whether digital technologies are creating spaces and opportunities for workers to flourish as human beings capable of contributing to the good of society.

At the level of norms, Kant's categorical imperatives offer plausible general principles. However, there is a large gap between these principles and specific norms that could inform decision making. For example, in the famous "Moral Machine" experiment (Awad et al., 2018), people were asked to decide on different scenarios encountered by a self-driving car with a brake failure: in the event of an unavoidable collision, should the car harm a passenger or a pedestrian? Does it matter if pedestrians are elderly? What if they are workers or homeless? Thus, the principles of fairness and beneficence commonly associated with Kantian ethics (Gabriel, 2020) need other criteria to solve this kind of dilemma. In concrete real-life scenarios, there is a need for the adoption of new norms that can capture the challenges of the renewed workplace. These norms should be informed by experience and historical developments. This highlights the role of regulation in informing ethical decision making. This is particularly evident in the case of Uber, one of the most well-known of the new types of digitally enabled work[5] (known as "platform work", see Deganis et al., 2021), where tensions between regulatory efforts, workers' rights, and the economic interests of the platform have been in the headlines many times (e.g., Ram, 2018; Scheiber, 2021). In this context and in others involving new forms of work there is need to consider new regulations that ensure

[5] See Chap. 4 for a more detailed discussion.

that all relevant stakeholders' interests are accounted for. More generally, concrete norms are needed, norms that can only be developed through political debate and deliberation, in order to protect the relevant goods at stake in these new work contexts. Likewise, virtues are needed to ensure that norms are implemented properly.

A virtue is a human trait that enables a person to flourish and contribute to the good of society, enabling individuals to act well (Aristotle, 2000; Melé, 2009). Recent research has sought to relocate the tradition of virtues in the renewed technological context (Vallor, 2016; Rocchi, 2019), and there are publications which address the need to consider virtues when assessing specific digital technologies (e.g., Grodzinsky, 2017; Gal et al., 2020) or new modes of work enabled by technology (Rocchi & Bernacchio, 2022). The Cambridge Analytica scandal led many to consider how the extremely good potential of digital technologies (a social media platform and big data analytics) and the existence of norms that would protect consumers' privacy are still not enough to guarantee the achievement of societal good. While the Cambridge Analytica whistleblower disclosed this situation and made people aware of the misuse of data—showing the virtues of justice and courage—a myriad of similar situations on a smaller scale still expose our data to different kind of violations, and the development of the virtues in those responsible for this data would fill the gap in regulation enforcement (or, sometimes, even regulation gaps). For example, the exercise of the virtue of justice, defined as the habit of giving each person what is due to her, would help companies make appropriate use of the information they source from their clients. Thus, virtues enable individuals within organisations, not only to choose effective means within the constraints of a given regulatory framework but, more importantly, to ensure that regulations are implemented so that they support work that contributes to workers' personal flourishing and to the good of society. While acknowledging the importance of external goods as tangible outcome of work (e.g., salary, social status, reputation), the virtues enable the workers to consciously seek internal goods, that is, excellent work that contributes positively to society.

In conclusion, the presented agent-centred approach (typical of virtue ethics) would consider—simultaneously—the goodness of the outcome (*goods*), the norms necessary to avoid harm and facilitate cooperation for the good of society (*norms*), and the habits of those involved in the creation (and not just in the use) of digital technologies (*virtues*). It is important to clarify that the presented perspective does not intend to provide ready-made solutions, but it rather provides the intellectual tools to think about these issues in greater depth, appreciating the impact of digital technologies on the future of work.

10.4 Conclusions and Future Research

This chapter presents an overview of different ethical approaches and highlights how an agent-centred approach to ethics, based on goods, norms, and virtues, is the most suitable to analyse from an ethical point of view the impact of digital technologies on the future of work.

Further research can enrich the framework on the three levels. As for the goods, parameters to evaluate the goodness of a digital technology, including the goods of human flourishing and the common good, should be defined more clearly in this new context of digital work, by establishing metrics that can account for goodness within a company's decision-making process. At the level of norms, an analysis of incentives that encourage virtuous behaviours and discourage societal harm, and more generally, the regulations that can promote human flourishing in this new context, could be studied. The development of concrete norms deriving from general principles within the context of decision-making algorithms in AI-based technologies constitutes another area of further research at the level of norms. Finally, at the level of virtues, it can be explored how the cultivation of specific virtues favour the development of workers' human flourishing and enhance their willingness to meaningfully contribute to the good of society. More generally, a reconsideration of a theory of action that takes into account the object, end, and circumstances of the action performed within the renewed technological and organisational context would be welcomed.

References

Annas, J. (1995). *The morality of happiness* (1st ed.). Oxford University Press.

Aranzadi, J. (2011). The possibilities of the acting person within an institutional framework: Goods, norms, and virtues. *Journal of Business Ethics, 99*(1), 87–100.

Aristotle. (2000). *Nicomachean ethics* (Cambridge Texts in the History of Philosophy). Cambridge University Press.

Awad, E., Dsouza, S., Kim, R., Schulz, J., Henrich, J., Shariff, A., Bonnefon, J.-F., & Rahwan, I. (2018). The moral machine experiment. *Nature, 563*(7729), 59–64.

Balliester, T., & Elsheikhi, A. (2018). The future of work: A literature review. *International Labour Organization Working Papers, 29.*

Baron, M., Pettit, P., & Slote, M. (1997). *Three methods of ethics: A debate* (Great Debates in Philosophy). Blackwell.

Bertolaso, M., & Rocchi, M. (2022). Specifically human: Human work and care in the age of machines. *Business Ethics: A European Review, 31*(3), 888–898.

Browning, K. (2021). Microsoft will make augmented reality headsets for the army in a $21.9 billion deal. *The New York Times*, March 31. https://www.nytimes.com/2021/03/31/business/microsoft-army-ar.html

Brusoni, S., & Vaccaro, A. (2017). Ethics, technology and organizational innovation. *Journal of Business Ethics, 143*(2), 223–226.

Capone, L., Rocchi, M., & Bertolaso, M. (forthcoming). Rethinking 'Digital': A Genealogical Enquiry into the Meaning of Digital and Its Impact on Individuals and Society. AI & Society.

Deganis, I., Tagashira, M., & Yang, W. (2021). *Digitally enabled new forms of work and policy implications for labour regulation frameworks and social protection systems.* United Nations Department of Economic and Social Affairs, Policy Brief 113.

Floridi, L., Cowls, J., Beltrametti, M., Chatila, R., Chazerand, P., Dignum, V., Luetge, C., et al. (2018). AI4People—An ethical framework for a good AI society: Opportunities, risks, principles, and recommendations. *Minds and Machines*, November.

Gabriel, I. (2020). Artificial Intelligence, values, and alignment. *Minds and Machines, 30*(3), 411–437.

Gal, U., Jensen, T. B., & Stein, M.-K. (2020). Breaking the vicious cycle of algorithmic management: A virtue ethics approach to people analytics. *Information and Organization, 30*(2), 100301.

Grodzinsky, F. S. (2017). Why Big Data needs the virtues. In T. M. Powers (Ed.), *Philosophy and computing* (Philosophical Studies Series) (pp. 221–234). Springer International Publishing.

Hooker, B. (2000). *Ideal code, real world: A rule-consequentialist theory of morality.* Oxford University Press.

Hursthouse, R. (1999). *On virtue ethics.* Oxford University Press.

Jasanoff, S. (2016). *The ethics of invention: Technology and the human future* (The Norton Global Ethics Series) (1st ed.). W.W. Norton & Company.

Kant, I. (2012). *Groundwork of the metaphysics of morals* (Cambridge Texts in the History of Philosophy) (Rev. ed.). Cambridge University Press.

Lee, D. (2019). Microsoft staff: Do not use HoloLens for war. *BBC News*, February 22. https://www.bbc.com/news/technology-47339774

Lynn, T., Mooney, J. G., Rosati, P., & Fox, G. (Eds.). (2020). *Measuring the business value of cloud computing* (Palgrave Studies in Digital Business and Enabling Technologies). Palgrave Macmillan.

MacIntyre, A. C. (1992). Plain persons and moral philosophy: Rules, virtues and goods. *The American Catholic Philosophical Quarterly, 66*(1), 3–19.
MacIntyre, A. C. (1999). *Dependent rational animals: Why human beings need the virtues.* Open Court.
MacIntyre, A. C. (2007). *After virtue: A study in moral theory* (3rd ed.). University of Notre Dame Press.
Melé, D. (2005). Ethical education in accounting: Integrating rules, values and virtues. *Journal of Business Ethics, 57*(1), 97–109.
Melé, D. (2009). *Business ethics in action: Seeking human excellence in organizations.* Palgrave Macmillan.
Moore, G. (2017). *Virtue at work: Ethics for individuals, managers and organizations.* Oxford University Press.
Parfit, D. (1984). *Reasons and persons.* Clarendon Press.
Ram, A. (2018). Uber faces tough new regulations in London. *Financial Times,* February 15. https://www.ft.com/content/3796d1e0-124c-11e8-8cb6-b9ccc4c4dbbb
Rhonheimer, M. (2011). *The perspective of morality: Philosophical foundations of thomistic virtue ethics.* Catholic University of America Press.
Rocchi, M. (2019). Technomoral Financial Agents: The Future of Ethics in the Fintech Era. *Finance and Common Good*, 46–47, 25–42.
Rocchi, M., & Bernacchio, C. (2022). The virtues of Covid-19 pandemic: How working from home can make us the best (or the worst) version of ourselves. *Business and Society Review, 127*(3), 685–700.
Russo, F. (2018). Digital technologies, ethical questions, and the need of an informational framework. *Philosophy & Technology, 31*(4), 655–667.
Scanlon, T. M. (2011). How I Am Not a Kantian. In D. Parfit (Ed.), *On What Matters: Volume Two,* (pp. 116–139). Oxford University Press.
Scheiber, N. (2021). Uber and lyft ramp up legislative efforts to shield business model. *The New York Times,* June 9. https://www.nytimes.com/2021/06/09/business/economy/uber-lyft-gig-workers-new-york.html.
Schwab, K. (2016). *The fourth industrial revolution* (1st ed.). Crown Business.
Schwab, K., & Davis, N. (2018). *Shaping the future of the fourth industrial revolution: A guide to building a better world* (1st ed.). Currency.
Sison, A., & Fontrodona, J. (2012). The common good of the firm in the Aristotelian-Thomistic tradition. *Business Ethics Quarterly, 22*(2), 211–246.
Vallor, S. (2016). *Technology and the virtues: A philosophical guide to a future worth wanting.* Oxford University Press.

Index

T. Lynn et al. (eds.), *The Future of Work*, Palgrave Studies in Digital Business & Enabling Technologies,
https://doi.org/10.1007/978-3-031-31494-0

Milton Keynes UK
Ingram Content Group UK Ltd.
UKHW021835131124
450975UK00004B/65

9 783031 314933